THE TEN-SECOND
MIRACLE

GAY HENDRICKS, PH.D.

THE TEN-SECOND MIRACLE

*Creating
Relationship
Breakthroughs*

HarperSanFrancisco
A Division of HarperCollins*Publishers*

HarperCollins books may be purchased for educational, business, or sales promotional use. For information please write: Special Markets Department, HarperCollins Publishers, Inc., 10 East 53rd Street, New York, NY 10022.

HarperCollins Web Site: http://www.harpercollins.com

HarperCollins®, 📖 ®, and HarperSanFrancisco™ are trademarks of HarperCollins Publishers Inc.

FIRST EDITION

[First HarperSanFrancisco edition published 1998]

Library of Congress Cataloging-in-Publication Data

Hendricks, Gay.

   The ten second miracle: creating relationship breakthroughs / Gay Hendricks. —1st ed.

   p.   cm.

   ISBN 0–06–251489-X (cloth)

   ISBN 0–06–tk (pbk.)

   1. Interpersonal conflict. 2. Interpersonal relations. I. Title.

BF637.I48H46

158.2—dc21   98–12440

                                                                              CIP

98 99 00 01 02 ❖/RRD 10 9 8 7 6 5 4 3 2 1

To Kathlyn, who blesses everything she touches

CONTENTS

ACKNOWLEDGMENTS

The support of friends, family, and colleagues from across the land and down through the years has made my journey richer than they could ever imagine. I thank: David Hubbard, Kenny and Julia Loggins, Carl Thoresen, John Krumboltz, Andrew Weil, Bonnie Raitt, Barry Weinhold, Leo Zeff, Dwight Webb, Mary Manin Morrissey, Gary Zukav, John Bradshaw, and Jim Fadiman.

I am very grateful to the wonderful people who gave me their miracle stories to use in this book. Although I changed your names and other identifying details, you know who you are and how much I appreciate you.

To my students, whom I've always regarded as fellow seekers, all I can say is: I couldn't have done it without you. I'll be forever moved by the thousands of hours of labor-of-love enthusiasm you brought to the task.

I am blessed to have a great support team. I feel particularly grateful for the steady and sunny presence of the director of our institute, Gail Padilla, an inspiring young woman of great creativity and resourcefulness.

To Mark Chimsky and Diane Gedymin, deep gratitude for your kindness to me and so many authors.

To my miraculous literary agent, Sandy Diykstra, thanks for the ten-year miracle.

I have some very good news: You are never more than ten seconds away from a breakthrough in the most important area of your life. I base this news on careful study of more than three thousand sessions in which real people healed real relationship problems. When you make five specific moves—none taking longer than ten seconds— you will see relationship miracles occur before your eyes.

A Powerful Moment of Discovery

The Ten-Second Miracle began for me one day when I watched a woman change her relationship destiny before my eyes. It took her only ten seconds to do it, and that magic moment changed my life as well as hers. Join me in my office as we relive that moment together:

Jan slumps in her chair, her face a mask of sadness, depression, and confusion. She says she's just broken up with her boyfriend, and he's more than a boyfriend, he's a trend. It's the fourth time this year she's gotten excited about a new relationship, only to have it crash and burn or wither and die. At age 31, she's beginning to despair about her fate: "What's this all about?" she wonders. "Why can't I find someone?"

She goes on to tell me a riveting detail. This breakup feels particularly awful because she had just attended a workshop about creating your ideal mate. One of the workshop activities was to make a list of all the qualities you were looking for in a mate. Her list contained more than thirty items. A man had shown up in her life rather quickly after the workshop, and he represented many of her ideals. So, when this "ideal" relationship blew up and ended, she was devastated.

After hearing all this, I pose a question to her. This is a question so powerful that I have to be careful when to ask it. If people aren't ready for it, the question sails over their head. But I sense the timing is right, so I say: "When you think about all of this—the breakup, this trend, this despair—what about it do you have the most trouble facing and accepting?"

She draws a big breath and lets it out. Her eyes take on a faraway look.

"The hardest thing to accept is that I might be alone all my life."

I nod. "Then let's face that right now. Go ahead and feel that aloneness, that fear, that possibility."

"But I don't want to feel that way, even for a second!"

"I know you don't, but you'll live in fear of that aloneness until you let yourself *consciously* feel it. Feel it for as long as it takes to come to terms with it."

She sits upright as the truth of my statement sinks in. She closes her eyes, and her face takes on a look of rapt attentiveness.

At that moment I happen to look at the second hand of the clock. I notice that she stays in that rapt state of focus for ten seconds. Suddenly her eyes pop open.

"I just got what you mean," she says, with genuine excitement in her voice. *"I've been alone because I was afraid to let myself feel alone. I've been avoiding that feeling since I was a kid.* I had to keep creating and re-creating it because I wouldn't let myself feel it. That's *it!"*

And that apparently *was* it, because the most remarkable thing happened in the following week. She called to say she had met a new man "out of the blue." She couldn't keep her next appointment because he had invited her to go sailing with him for a week at his family's summer cabin. I have never seen her again in person, although I have heard from her often over the years since then. In the following order, here is what I've received from her: a postcard from the sailing trip, a wedding invitation later in the year, a birth announcement two years later, and a holiday letter each year since.

I call that a miracle.

I've thought of that moment many times in the years since it happened. A glance at the second hand of a clock put an idea into my mind that sent me on a lifelong quest. In that moment I first began to wonder: Does any great change in our lives ever take longer than ten seconds? That observation led to the twenty-some years of observation that this book rests on, and to the discovery of the five key miracles that transform relationships. I'll have more to say about the research later on, but first I want to share with you another powerful moment, one

that happened just recently. Join me again in my Santa
Barbara office:

Sally and Jim glare at each other from separate chairs in my
office. They have been married fourteen years, have three children and two successful careers. They are impeccably dressed
and carry themselves with assurance. To the outside world all
might look well, but their body language tells a different story,
a tale of betrayal and deceit. They've been at an impasse for
weeks, and finally they've sought help.

His fists clench repeatedly; her arms are tightly crossed.
Their chests strain in that labored way I call fight-or-flight
breathing. My first half-hour with them has been tense—the air
is electric with blame, defensiveness, and denial. Now they've
ground to a temporary halt, and I am about to seize the
moment with a bold move.

I lean forward and get their attention.

"Would you both be willing to solve this problem? Right
here? Right now?" I don't know exactly what the problem is yet,
but I know for certain that nothing will shift until they drop
blaming each other and make a commitment to healing this
wound in their marriage. I know that commitment is always the
place to start, no matter how long the struggle has gone on.

They blink and stare at me. He says, "Well, would we be here
if we weren't willing to solve the problem?" I explain that, unfortunately, many people come to relationship counseling just to
go through the motions. They already know they want to leave,
or they're just looking for confirmation that their spouse really
is a jerk. So, just being here isn't enough, I say. You've got to be
here *and* make a commitment to solving the problem.

They take a moment to digest this. Finally, she says yes. He nods and says yes. Their body language indicates despair and doubt, but at least their mouths have said yes. That's enough to get us started.

Now for the moment of truth.

> ME: *There are only two things that can get people as stuck as you are. One: There's something you don't want to feel. Two: There's something you're afraid to say.* A lot of people will sacrifice their health and their happiness to avoid feeling something they don't want to feel. A lot of others will sacrifice themselves and the relationship they're in to avoid saying some truth they've been hiding.

I wait until they make straight-on eye contact with me, then I ask:

"What is it that you've been afraid to feel?

"What is it that you've been afraid to say?"

Their reaction when they hear the questions tells me all I need to know. He squirms and licks his lips. She wrinkles her brow critically and looks off into the distance. Because I've had thirty years of observing body language, I can tell he feels guilty about something, and she's pretending not to know something her intuition has told her long ago.

> ME: Jim, to me you look guilty about something. Sally, you looked off into the distance when I asked those questions.

> JIM: Wait a minute, why pick on me?

> SALLY: I thought he was picking on *me*.

> ME: Jim, Sally, I notice you're getting defensive rather than

talking about anything you might feel guilty about or anything you're avoiding.

Jim snorts, and Sally's head whips around to look at him. Her eyes are wide in what looks like surprise or fear.

ME: What is it you don't want to feel? What is it you're avoiding saying?

Suddenly the energy shifts in the room as both of them take a deeper breath. I can tell that someone is dropping the facade and facing what's real. Jim tucks his chin to his chest and closes his eyes. Sally looks at him searchingly.

JIM: *I can't stand it anymore, all this hiding. I've gotta tell you . . . I slept with another woman and I went to see a lawyer.*

SALLY (letting out an angry bark of laughter): *I knew it, I knew it, I knew it.*

She starts to cry; he chews his bottom lip and stares at the carpet.

ME: You've been hiding all this, Jim, and Sally, you've been avoiding knowing what your intuition has been telling you. When did this happen, Jim?

JIM: Three months ago.

Sally spins around and stomps her feet in a rage.

....

Let me pause there and ask, Does this sound like a potential miracle to you? If you said no, I can relate: It didn't at first to me, either. But let me tell you what happened next. After this potent revelation, they spent an intense ten minutes discharging anger and tears. After ten minutes the intensity subsided. You may find that hard to believe, but I have found that when people give themselves permission to feel their emotions deeply, even the heaviest emotions blow through quickly, like summer rainstorms. When fully embraced, the storms of feeling seldom last ten minutes. Of course, if we don't give ourselves permission to feel, the cloud of those same emotions may hang over our heads for years.

Following their outbursts, I invited them to take separate walks around the block outside my office. I wanted them to have some breathing space, and a ten-minute walk is a good way to get it. I've used this technique many times—it shifts people into a different state of consciousness. I asked them to focus, during their walk, on the question I'd asked earlier: Are you willing to solve this problem?

When they returned, everything had changed. Both of them were standing taller, looking stronger.

> SALLY: If you want out of the marriage, let's go ahead and get a divorce. *I'm angry at you for lying to me, but I don't want to stay in this kind of marriage for five minutes longer.*

> JIM: Well, if that's what you want to do, okay, but I've realized that what I did was incredibly stupid. I suddenly realized why I did it. *I don't really want another relationship. I think I was just so frustrated I went on autopilot. I hate the way our lives have been going.*

When Sally hears this, the anger drains out of her face; she looks interested.

SALLY: What do you mean?

JIM: Working our tails off to stay ahead of the game—getting so into orthodontia and soccer practice and all that. We haven't had a glass of wine or a close talk together in I-don't-know-how-long. We have sex once a week, but we haven't made love in a year.

SALLY: Yeah. I don't disagree.

This was the beginning of a profound change in their marriage. Let me jump ahead to another ten-second pivot point in our fourth session together:

ME: Does either of you have an idea yet of why you created this problem right now in your lives?

JIM: Explain.

ME: Well, usually people will manufacture some huge problem in their relationships because they're afraid to confront some issue deep down inside themselves.

SALLY: Oh, I see what you mean. Like, *why did I set it up to have the man in my life get interested in another woman?*

JIM: Or like, *why did I need to create a big drama with Sally? What was I avoiding looking at inside myself?*

ME: Right.

JIM: *Hmm, I had a dream I was dying the other night. I was drowning in a puddle that was only a couple of inches deep.*

ME: What does that mean to you?

JIM: All this stuff we keep ourselves busy with—three cars and braces for the kids' teeth and getting the pets vaccinated. I mean, I know it's all important and everything, but it just seems . . . like it's taking over my life.

SALLY (snorts): And don't forget the plumbing. (They had just spent thousands of dollars repairing burst pipes at their vacation cabin.)

JIM: Yeah.

ME: Take a moment to feel whatever feelings you have about all that taking over your lives.

They both take a few deep breaths.

JIM: *Angry. Angry and sad.*

SALLY: Yeah, *me too.*

ME: I know it's painful, but there's something here that really gives me hope. You're both on the same wavelength, feeling those same feelings. You've become allies.

SALLY: Instead of enemies.

Jim nods in wonderment.

There's a long way to go and much more to do, but now I know they'll get there. When people link up behind a common goal—whether it's re-creating a marriage or walking on the surface of the moon—nothing can stop them.

We Need to Know Miracles Are Possible

We all need to know that relationship miracles like this not only are possible but also can be produced reliably. We need to know that we can bridge the chasms between our own hearts and the hearts of others. We need to know there's a way to break up the logjams of love.

Sometimes the miracle is in our relationship with ourselves. Listen in on another conversation:

A woman stands before me with a pained look on her face.

"I shouldn't be here," she says. "I should be home in bed with this migraine."

"When did you first feel it?" I ask.

She thinks for a moment. "Last night after dinner."

An internist might ask what she ate, but I am concerned with internals of a different sort.

"What Ten-Second truth did you fail to say just before you started getting the headache?"

This question catches her by surprise, and she lets out a bark of harsh laughter.

"*I saw my husband heading into the den to watch TV, without thanking me for cooking dinner, and leaving me with all the dishes to do. And I knew I didn't have guts enough to ask him to help me.*"

"What were you afraid would happen if you asked?"

"*I'm afraid he'd tell me it's the last straw and walk out the door.*"

"What would you have said if you'd had the courage? What would the Ten-Second statement be?"

"Probably '*Hey, you wash the dishes for once!*' Or maybe '*Let's do the dishes together, like we used to.*'"

Her eyes are starting to moisten, but I notice a softening of her face and a relaxation of her shoulders.

"How's your migraine now?"

"Gone."

....

In my book, that's a miracle.

We Need Miracles in Our Close Relationships

There is no doubt we need miracles: In every corner of the world, relationship conflict is the single biggest drain on creative energy. If we can find reliable ways to break up the logjams of love, we will have plenty of energy to solve the other problems we face on our planet. My experiences over the past twenty-five years have led me to believe strongly in the creative potential of human beings. The Ten-Second Miracle is designed to rechannel the energy of conflict into creativity and love. When we can move quickly from the frozen wasteland of emotional distance to the warmth of a loving embrace, that's a miracle. Although I've now witnessed this miracle many times, I am still deeply moved by it every time.

The Ten-Second Miracle is designed to change the worst of feelings into the best of feelings. Let me tell you exactly what I mean.

The Worst of Feelings, the Best of Feelings

You have felt it. So have I. Some say it's the worst feeling in the world. There are two times when we feel it most painfully:

You are alone and you don't want to be. You feel the urge to be with somebody, but there is nobody around. You feel the urge to do something, but there is nothing you really want to do. You feel a pit in your stomach that no food could fill. A fist grips your chest, a tension that no trip to the gym can relax.

This feeling is awful, but I think another one may be even worse: You are with someone *physically* but alone in your heart.

You are in a room with someone you care about. It could be a first date or your mate of thirty years. It could even be a co-worker. You feel a tension between the two of you. You do not feel the easy flow of good feeling that connected you perhaps only moments before. Now you sense a distance, a wariness of each other—as if a collective breath is held between you. You yearn for the sweet ease of flow between you, but it is gone.

Wherever did it go? And can you ever get it back?

I call this feeling *the grip of longing.* You long for connection and don't feel it. Frequently, the other person feels the same painful yearning. But because we usually hide the grip of longing with anger or confusion or silence or a happy mask, neither of you can appreciate that you are both in the grip of the same deeper feeling.

As the silence grows thicker, you notice a familiar sensation in your chest. Instead of the open feeling of warmth and flow that lets you know all is well, now you feel a constriction—a fist in the chest. As the seconds tick by, the fist tightens and the gripping spreads through your body. A despair begins to settle over you. Soon it sours your thoughts and your mood. You think: No matter what I've accomplished in my life, nothing means anything as long as I'm in the grip of this feeling. It is the worst feeling in the world.

Then, a miracle occurs.

You reach down inside and search your feelings. You realize you feel tight in the belly and heavy in the chest. You take a deep breath and blurt out the simple truth of your feelings. What you say takes less than ten seconds but changes the whole tone of the moment:

"I'm scared," you say. "I'm sad. I want to connect with you." The moment you speak this stark truth, the fist that grips your body loosens—a flow of positive sensation begins. A look of surprise and interest comes over the other person's face. Within ten seconds you feel a new sensation of spaciousness through your body. You feel ease returning to the relationship. The other person smiles and relaxes. You are reconnected, and life works again.

When this happens—when you feel an easeful flow of good feeling returning to your body or to a relationship—it is a wonderful moment. *When you break free of the* grip of longing *and ease into the* flow of love, *it is the best feeling in the world.* I've felt it myself on many joyful occasions, and my heart has warmed as it happened in front of me in hundreds of therapy sessions. Because I have felt the power of this moment, and because I know a reliable way to help it happen, I feel deeply optimistic about our future.

I want everyone to know how to produce this miracle in his or her life. If we can learn that we have the power to re-create love in our lives reliably, we hold keys to our own happiness and to the future of human evolution.

The Essential Discovery

The Ten-Second Miracles are *not* insights or attitudes—they are body-mind shifts as easy as shifting your eyes to look at the horizon. The techniques are effortless—in fact, they are so natural that it requires effort to *resist* doing them.

More than twenty-five years of work with many thousands of people has given me a deep and unshakable confidence in the power of the techniques I will share with you. Because of this experience, I know in my bones that you can reliably produce relationship breakthroughs to get what you need in the most important area of your life. And when I talk about breakthroughs, I'm talking about moments like these:

> You are walking along the street, feeling slightly "off." You know you're not ill, but something's wrong and you're not sure what. You'd love to find a quick way to get a flow of organic good feeling moving again inside you.

You need a Ten-Second Miracle. It was designed and carefully tested for just such moments—it will release a flow of good feeling in you, and it will do it reliably.

> You focus your awareness on the place in your body that feels most stuck. You rest your awareness there and simply pay attention to yourself, as if listening nonjudgmentally to yourself. You take a few deep breaths and stay present to the feelings in your body. Suddenly a flow of good feeling courses through you, like the awakening of a welcome breeze on a still day. The off-center feeling disappears, replaced by a calm sense of well-being.

This is the Ten-Second Miracle at work. It works reliably, and it's always there when you need it.

Solving Two Problems

The Ten-Second Miracle solves two problems we face nearly every day of our lives:

1. How to feel a flow of good feeling *inside* ourselves, and how to open the flow when it has become dammed up.

2. How to feel the flow of love and good feeling *between us and other people* we care about, and how to release the flow when it has been blocked.

These two problems become worse the closer we are to ourselves and to one another. In other words, the better you know yourself, the less you can tolerate blockages to the flow of your good feeling. The same is true in relationships: The closer we are to other people, the less we can tolerate the distance and stuckness that comes into the best of relationships from time to time.

The Benefit

The great benefit of the Ten-Second Miracle is that it provides a reliable way to open the flow of loving feeling. I know from personal experience, and from studying evidence from more than three thousand counseling sessions, that it is possible to feel the flow of loving feeling—inside our bodies and between us and others—nearly all the time. I cannot say all the time, because I'm not there yet and don't know anybody who is. Once I discovered the Ten-Second Miracle, though, I began spending more and more time enjoying the flow of good feeling inside and the flow of love with others. Sometimes, whole years can go by without an unpleasant word being spoken in my marriage. Since I come from a family in which I never saw a happy marriage, to have created one seems beyond miraculous to me. Perhaps more important, though, we now know what it takes to release the blockage of loving feeling. We now have a reliable technology for reawakening love.

Why the Ten-Second Miracle Is Important

The Ten-Second Miracle is important to every person, whether at home or at work, alone or with loved ones. If you do not know *a conscious move* to make during the ten-second windows that create your destiny, your uncon-scious programming imprints these moments with your old patterns. Then, these patterns recycle and escalate as the relationship proceeds. A template formed during an initial meeting of two people can produce distress decades later.

A Miraculous Observation

Since entering the healing professions in 1968, I have had the privilege and pleasure of working directly with more than twenty thousand people in individual, relation-ship, and group sessions. In addition, I trained approxi-mately twelve hundred therapists in the twenty-one years that I was a professor in the counseling psychology depart-ment at the University of Colorado. My particular area of interest is in helping people make rapid shifts in the qual-ity of their relationships. From these experiences, I have access to notes and videotapes from several thousand ses-sions, showing every form of conflict resolution and rela-tionship breakthrough of which I'm aware.

Earlier I mentioned my realization that a profound shift I'd witnessed was because of a ten-second move my client made. As I began to look with fresh eyes, I made the dis-covery I will share with you in this book: There would come a moment—a window of opportunity—and when certain things happened in that window, there was an immediate shift toward harmony and resolution. I carried out further observations in my own life, in sessions done by my graduate students, and in the corporate world where I often do consultations with executives. I could see the same phenomenon at work there as well. Over the next few years I went on a quest: I bought a stopwatch and began studying videotapes. I set aside my previous theories and approached the enterprise with a beginner's mind. I soon discovered that the Ten-Second phenomenon applied across boundaries of gender, sex, race, and culture. There were many different types of relationships on the videos. The majority involved heterosexual married couples, but more than two hundred homosexual relationships were represented, as well as several hundred minority, multiracial, and multicultural relationships. Through this process, I confirmed the remarkable discovery that shifted my whole perspective: The moments when relationships change for the better occur in *ten-second windows* when specific moves are made. The moves are based on specific laws of relationship that became obvious as the videotapes revealed their secrets.

Within ten seconds of the move, positive shifts would reliably happen. When I say "shifts," I mean specific things like these:

- Moods brighten.

- Tensions melt.

- Impasses dissolve, and problems move toward resolution.

- People take deeper breaths.

- Facial expressions soften and tight shoulders drop.

- People make friendly eye contact with each other. They often reach out and touch each other within ten seconds.

Teaching the Moves

As I studied the videotapes, I was continually surprised by one finding: It's never insights that change lives. For example, people's lives don't change if they realize their parents didn't love them right. Rather, the things that change people's lives are simple moves—specific things they do. That's why we can teach them with precision. They are crystal-clear and require no jargon.

Five simple moves change people's lives, and we will work with these moves carefully and extensively in this book. To begin, though, let me tell you the five powerful secrets that the Ten-Second Miracle rests on.

You'll see dramatic positive changes in your relationships when you:

- Pause for ten seconds to feel—*deeply* feel—what is going on inside you. You might carry a sadness inside you for decades, but it doesn't shift until you pause to resonate with it consciously for those ten magic seconds.

- Speak a particular type of simple truth. The truths that heal relationships are usually statements of fact, such as "I saw Mary again last week," or statements of feeling, such as "I'm scared of being alone." Moreover, the truths that change people's lives can be spoken in less than ten seconds, using only one breath.

The feeling statements that change people's lives usually point to sensations from three *feeling zones* of the body: chest, belly, neck/shoulders. Sometimes the truth is an "I notice" statement, as in "I notice when you said you were going to the office you rubbed the back of your neck."

- Claim responsibility for something that you've previously felt victimized by. The breakthrough occurs the moment you say, "I take full responsibility for what went wrong in my marriage," while simultaneously giving room for the other person to take full responsibility. The type of responsibility that heals people's lives never, ever involves blame.

- Face and accept something that has been avoided or denied. You spend ten seconds in the full-body embrace of some reality you've been avoiding. It could be a feeling you've been avoiding, such as despair, anger, or fear. Or it could be an event in your life you haven't wanted to face. The moment we open our arms to whatever is real, our hearts begin to heal.

- Shift from worry to wonder. Life changes the moment we start wondering about the things we think we know. You may know beyond a shadow of a doubt that you were colossally wronged in a particular relationship, but your life won't change until you shift to wondering, What was my part in that drama? How and why did I invite that into my life?

Do these things and you will see miracles unfold before your eyes. I'm not exaggerating.

Teachable Skills

I found that these moves could be readily learned by my clients. When they used them, amazing changes occurred so rapidly I could hardly believe it. I began to call them Ten-Second Miracles, because of their effect on relationships. When people used the Miracle Moves, their relationships took quantum jumps toward health and happiness. By contrast, relationship *distress would appear within ten seconds* after one of the rules was violated or misapplied. Over the past ten years I have shifted my practice and professional trainings to teach these Miracle Moves. Now my colleagues and I have amassed enough data to share the information with you.

The Conscious Moment

We can all probably recall *unconscious moments* when something was said or done that destroyed the flow of intimacy between us and a key person in our lives. By contrast, knowing the ten-second windows and the Miracle Moves allows us to have *conscious moments*. Conscious moments are breakthroughs when we do or say something that opens a new horizon in a relationship. We step through into a new zone of possibility, one we haven't seen before. And the good news is: We are always only ten seconds away from a conscious moment.

Simplifying the Most Complex Area of Living

Learning what to do during the ten-second windows brings simplicity and order to your life. These days, many people are concerned with simplifying their lives—books on the subject are proliferating. No one, however, has addressed how to simplify the most complicating factor of our lives: relationships. Relationship conflicts sap our energy and clutter our minds with excess noise. In this book, I will not only tell you the major rules for creating miracles in your relationships; I will show you exactly how to spot the ten-second windows when they're easiest to do. You will have a pocketful of miracles you can carry with you everywhere.

Examples of Miracles

My favorite dictionary definition says that a "miracle" is something that evokes marvel and wonder. I have witnessed and documented hundreds of relationship breakthroughs that I would not hesitate to call miracles. See if you agree that these events qualify as miracles:

- A man made a commitment to marriage immediately after one of the Ten-Second Miracle Moves, even though he had steadfastly avoided the subject for three years. In other words, his girlfriend made a specific communication that took less than ten seconds, and he immediately shifted off his "no commitment" position.

- A woman had a completely satisfying sexual experience with her husband after she made one of the Ten-Second moves. By doing so she broke a seven-year nonorgasmic drought. On the surface, the actual communication had nothing to do with sex, but it immediately affected the quality of her sexual intimacy.

* Two former business partners dropped an expensive lawsuit the same day they applied one of the Ten-Second moves, ending a six-month struggle between them.

* A three-generational family conflict dissolved seconds after one person uncrossed her arms, let go of her stance of indignation, and made a Ten-Second Communication, "I'm feeling so sad." Within seconds I witnessed a genuine marvel—two people who hadn't spoken to each other in a long time were sobbing in each other's arms.

The Mega-Rule

As people learn to make specific moves during the ten-second windows, their relationships improve remarkably. Here, then, is what I call the Mega-Rule:

RELATIONSHIPS FLOURISH OR WITHER IN TEN-SECOND WINDOWS OF COMMUNICATION. *EVERY TRULY IMPORTANT RELATIONSHIP COMMUNICATION TAKES LESS THAN TEN SECONDS.* YOUR POWER AND WELL-BEING FLOW FROM *INITIATING* THOSE TEN-SECOND COMMUNICATIONS, NOT WAITING FOR THEM TO HAPPEN.

A Universal Problem and a Universal Solution

Relationships are destroyed by ignoring specific moments that should be noticed and handled within ten seconds. *When you handle the moments correctly, you get what you need* in your relationships. It is urgent to know what these moments are and how to handle each one.

Speaking Personally

I believe the Ten-Second Miracle saved my life. I was on the fast track to oblivion when I first felt the power of the work I'll share with you in this book. In 1969 I weighed more than three hundred pounds (a hundred and twenty pounds heavier than I weighed this morning); I was also a two-pack-a-day smoker with a cough that wouldn't go away. I had a crummy job and was stuck in an awful relationship. I was 24 years old.

Then . . .

By grace or just good luck, I got a second chance and took it. Within a year of waking up to the power of the Ten-Second Miracle, I lost a hundred pounds, freed myself from addiction, and broke out of the troubled relationship. Miraculously, my eyesight even improved after I began to change my life. Although I'd worn strong corrective lenses since third grade, I was able to pass my driving test without glasses within a year after my wake-up experience. My inner vision also opened and my life path became clear to me, allowing me to find my way to the career I love to this day.

We Create Who We Are Every Moment

My experience has shown me this: If we find a way to break out of the constriction, we free ourselves to feel the flow of love. If we know a way to move through the impasses of intimacy, we have a treasure beyond price. If we cannot—if we give up in the grip of constriction—our heart dies a little. If we turn away and resign to facing it again another day, a part of us always wonders: Will another day ever come?

We become who we are in how we handle moments of potential intimacy. Let me make this point even stronger: We shape the course of our lives by moments in which we open to intimacy or shrink away from it. We create our destiny by how we deal with the grip of longing. Unfortunately for many of us, we sentence ourselves to destinies of loneliness and lack of fulfillment. By not knowing which way to turn at the crucial crossroads of destiny that confront us hourly, we lose our way and often do not get back home again.

You and I are not alone in this. I believe that everyone feels the grip of longing. My work has taken me around the world more than thirty times, and I have yet to see a culture in which the grip of longing is not part of daily life. The only difference is in how we deal with it.

How do you deal with the grip of longing? Do you strike out in anger? Do you give up? Do you reach for the remote control . . . or a box of chocolates? The way we relax the fist in our chest tells us, and the world, who we are. If you relax the fist and connect with other people, you become happy and free and productive. If you don't, nothing you accomplish and nothing you buy will ever fill the void.

I want to give you a gift I know will change your life. Through observation—particularly through thousands of hours of relationship therapy—I discovered something that radically changed my love life. Actually, it made my whole life possible. Since discovering it, my relationships have become easy, creative, and full of delight. My marriage to Kathlyn is richer with love than my wildest dreams could have predicted.

The gift is this: There are a few incredibly simple things you can do to release the grip of longing. When you relax its grip, you feel the flow of love again. Each of these simple things takes less than ten seconds. The mastery of them invites a lifetime of practice. I encourage you to make the mastery of them part of your life's purpose, so that you can make a relationship itself a path of artistic and spiritual development.

You Can Create a Positive Revolution Around You

The Ten-Second Miracles revolutionize the way people relate to one another. Once you begin practicing them, you will seem very different to other people, and they will be changed by their contact with you. Just yesterday, a woman said something that touched me deeply. It was the first day of a one-week relationship training that we hold several times a year at our center in Santa Barbara. We begin by having people introduce themselves and say a few sentences about what they want to accomplish during the training. A therapist said she had been to many workshops in various systems of relationship therapy. Each time she'd returned home, her husband, who is an accountant, had objected to the new language she was speaking and the new things she was advocating in their relationship. By contrast, she said, after taking our introductory training several months before, when she went back home her husband had a completely different reaction. He said, "I don't know what you did, but I want you to go do it some more. I want to do it, too. You're not using jargon or trying to teach me anything—you're just so changed that I want some of that for myself. Whatever you did, let's go do it together."

What she did was learn to use the Ten-Second Miracles. They don't require any jargon, and you don't have to preach their effectiveness to people. You just do them, and lives are changed as a result.

What we will do in our journey together is explore these simple things. I invite you to commit yourself body and soul for the short time it will take to gain access to the knowledge. I invite you to make an investment of time that has the power of bringing you a lifetime of easeful love. I invite you to practice these skills so that you can harvest the rich rewards that come with feeling the flow of love every day of your life.

My Promise to You

Here's my promise to you: If you use the Ten-Second Miracles in your life, you will experience three big benefits. You will probably experience a great many more benefits, but even if you only harvested the following three, I'm convinced you would find the endeavor worthwhile.

First, you will simplify the most complicated area of life—close relationships. The needless suffering caused by complicated relationship dramas consumes a tremendous amount of energy. In my experience, it's the single biggest drain of creative energy. Use the Miracles and you will feel more creative energy flowing through you than you have ever imagined.

Second, you will experience a very specific positive feeling in your body as you integrate the Miracles into your life. You will feel lighter all over, a flowing sense of ease in your body and a clarity in your mind. This feeling will replace the longing and fear that often have gripped our bodies so long we don't even feel the squeeze anymore. With practice, you'll discover that you can turn on that easeful flowing sensation in your body any time you want. You have to feel it to believe it.

Third, you will come to see that you have a great deal more power than you ever imagined. This is real power I'm talking about—you can feel it in your body all the time—not the illusory kind that comes and goes with money, promotions, and other status markers. In fact, you will discover that you are the source of miracles in your life, and that you can produce them reliably. It only takes one or two successful Miracle Moves to inspire a "Wow!" in you. Once you wow yourself, you are unstoppable. Soon you produce miracles everywhere you go. The feeling of self-confidence you get is life-changing for you and inspiring to others around you.

In our work together in this book, you will learn how to make the Miracle Moves so quickly and smoothly that you can do them in one breath. You will literally be one breath away from creating a miracle in the most significant area of your life.

Perhaps the best benefit is knowing that you are always only seconds away from producing benefits. All it takes is learning a few secrets and practicing a few simple techniques. It doesn't matter if you've been unhappy for decades . . . you are still only seconds away from the miracle. I can guarantee you that, and not just because I've seen it thousands of times. I can guarantee it because I know a secret. Once you understand it, you are ready for miracles.

The Secret

The secret is this: Our lives prosper or stagnate through moments of choice. There is no such thing as fate or destiny, not in the real world of relationship. We *create* our destiny with choices—often tiny choices—in tiny moments of time. We often overlook or forget or deny that we made a choice, but make no mistake about it: What we choose in those moments makes us who we are.

In particular, the choice-moments of close relationship have special power to shape our lives. I have been privileged to be in the presence of many people as they made choices that changed their destiny from suffering to happiness. I wish I could say it was always that way, but I have been deeply pained to be with others as they made choices that took them in the other direction. I want to do what I can to help you prevent unnecessary pain in your life.

Do You Really Need All That Pain?

Some people will tell you that pain is essential to help you forge your spirit. I am here to tell you that this notion is pure bunk. My experience over the past thirty years has shown me otherwise. *Some* pain is essential and useful to your life's learning, but most pain is of no value whatsoever and doesn't teach anybody anything. It is simply caused by poor choices at crucial moments. If you learn to keep your eyes open when you're driving a car, you can eliminate most of the pain you created when you were driving blindfolded. Learn to make the right choices at crucial moments and you can eliminate most of the pain from your life.

What you will have to do is learn to make simple Miracle Moves in those ten-second windows of intimacy that create your relationship destiny. And thank goodness you don't have to do it perfectly. If you miss a window, another one will come along shortly. In this book you will also learn what to do if you realize you missed a window.

Recognizing Ten-Second Windows

Let me show you what a ten-second window looks and sounds like. The following examples are drawn from actual problems I've seen people straighten out with the Miracle Moves we'll explore later. When you study ten-second windows carefully, you will see that they all follow the same pattern. Learn to recognize one and you are well on your way to knowing how all of them work. The first example happens so often in a given week we could hardly keep count of all the occurrences. I call them *moments of misunderstanding.*

I was teaching some of the material in this book to a group of advanced students. I had just made the point that if you miss a ten-second window and its corresponding Miracle Move, you can carry out a ten-minute "Heart-Talk" later to get back on track (the same Heart-Talk that's in part 3 of this book). I paused dramatically, then said, "And if you don't have the ten-minute conversation, you often create a ten-year problem." While the point sank in, I turned to change the flip-chart to the next page. When I faced the group again, I noticed a hurt and frightened look on the face of a woman in the front row. I said, "Donna, I notice something on your face. I'm wondering what you're feeling."

She said, with tears in her voice, "I find what you're saying so depressing. Bill and I have missed thousands of moments. I don't want to have to wait ten years to clear them up."

I realized she had misunderstood the whole point I had been making. She had taken my words to mean that she was doomed to ten years of misery because she'd missed the ten-second windows in which things could have been instantly put right. No wonder she found it depressing. Actually, however, I was saying the exact opposite, something immensely hopeful. I was saying that no matter how many ten-second windows you've missed, you can catch up in ten minutes, if you know what to do during those ten minutes.

She melted with relief when I clarified this point for her. She looked around the room and asked, "Did anyone else misunderstand this or was it just me?" It turned out she was the only person who had misunderstood. To her credit, she wondered aloud, "Why did I hear it like that, then?" She suddenly got an aha! look on her face and turned to her husband. "I just realized I heard it like that because I came in here tonight full of despair. I was listening for confirmation that things were hopeless between us."

They'd had an unpleasant encounter earlier in the day, and it remained unfinished. I asked them if they'd be willing to have a ten-minute Heart-Talk in the center of the room. I coached them through two Miracle Moves, and they cleared up the whole issue in closer to five minutes. It was miraculous to behold the radiance on their faces when they sat down again.

If I had not spotted the troubled look on Donna's face and paused to ask about it, she might have taken the despair home with her after the session. Had she not been courageous enough to speak authentically when I called her facial expression to her attention, she might have missed the breakthrough with her husband.

The ten-second window in this example occurred when I saw the expression on Donna's face and immediately paused to ask about it. Later in the book you will learn to call this a *feeling window.* I noticed signs of some feelings on her face and used a Ten-Second Miracle Move to deal with them. Moments like these happen all the time, and, unfortunately, most of them go unnoticed. As you become skilled at producing Ten-Second Miracles in your life, you will notice when things go "off" and take advantage of the ten-second window in which they can be easily fixed. A great deal of unnecessary misery is created by ignoring those opportunities.

The Components of Miracle Moves

As a prelude to learning about Miracle Moves later in the book, take a moment with me right now to study the move I made with Donna. Although seemingly simple, the two sentences I said to her contain the key to producing miracles every minute of your life. My first sentence was,

"Donna, I notice something on your face." My second sentence was, "I'm wondering what you're feeling."

Your Intention Produces the Miracle

It's the intention behind a Miracle Move that actually creates the miracle. My intentions were to notice and wonder and create an open space for harmony. My intentions were *not* to criticize Donna for what was on her face or to try to fix her. I was not making her wrong or making myself right—in other words, I wasn't running any agenda of mine over the top of hers. Contrast the way I handled this moment with typical moves you see every day. Faced with the same moment, many people would ignore the look on Donna's face. Even if they stopped to notice it, many would try to talk her out of whatever she was feeling. They would impose their own agenda on hers.

By saying "I notice something on your face," I simply held up an imaginary mirror to her, letting her know I had registered her reaction. This is one of the primary components of a Miracle Move: I call it "looking and seeing," and it can be contrasted with "ignoring." By not ignoring the obvious, I put myself squarely in touch with Donna's reality, and with reality itself. When we do this, we become safe in people's eyes—a person who is in touch with reality is always much safer than one who ignores reality.

Next, when I said "I wonder . . . ," I further opened a safe space for Donna to have the experience she was having. By speaking in "wonder-language," I was signaling my intention to help her make discoveries, not to make her wrong for anything she was feeling. This intention is a primary component of any Miracle Move. I call it "wondering," and it can be contrasted with "thinking we know." Almost all of us come from backgrounds where we were made wrong for our feelings. Almost all of us grew up around people who always thought they were right, who "thought they knew," and who were often devoid of genuine wonder. They often listened to our feelings through a filter of wanting our feelings to be different, as opposed to wondering about them. I later found that this was especially so for Donna—her background included physical as well as emotional abuse.

With two simple sentences, I created a safe space in which Donna could learn. It was a "shame-free" zone of pure possibility for discovery. She created the next miracle herself. Faced with the choice of hiding her feelings or revealing them, she made the crucial choice to reveal. The way she did it demonstrated other primary components of Miracle Moves. She *said what she was feeling* with no editing. Then, when she learned that she had misunderstood the idea, she *claimed ownership* of how she'd heard it (instead of blaming me for communicating it poorly). Then she *wondered* about why she'd heard it that way (instead of becoming defensive or distracting herself). In other words, she gave herself the same open space I had given her, and she was rewarded by a major self-discovery. All in a matter of moments.

I have seen thousands of such moments. That's why I can say with confidence: Your spiritual and psychological growth does not have to take time. It can happen virtually instantaneously if you adopt the correct intentions in your life. With enough practice, you do not even need external help—life itself becomes your teaching partner if you are open to learning from every moment.

A Moment of Unfairness

See if you can relate to the difficult situation I'm about to describe. There is a key situation that happens often in real life—I call it a *moment of unfairness.* Moments of unfairness put us in a bind that is hard to handle. Failure to deal skillfully with moments of unfairness probably causes us to consume more pain relievers than all the exercise classes in the world. The reason is this: For thousands of years, human beings have been registering *anger* in moments of unfairness. Someone takes advantage of us and we get angry at the trespass. But because the other person often has power over us, we swallow the anger instead of expressing it.

Let me give you a real-life example from a man who was learning how to use Ten-Second Miracles as part of couples counseling with his wife. His first big breakthrough happened at his office.

Kevin is a passionate soccer-dad. He ferries his kids to practice twice a week, never misses a game, and helps out the coach as often as he can. The majority of his social life with his wife revolves around activities with other soccer-parents. One afternoon at 5:30 he is straightening up his desk to leave for a game when his boss blazes in. He throws a sheaf of papers on Kevin's desk and says, "I'm about two hours away from closing the Sheaffer deal! I need you to review the paperwork and clear it for me before I take them out to dinner at 7:30. If it looks okay to you, we can get their signatures tonight."

Kevin says, "Oh, jeez, Ken, I can't. I've got my kids' soccer game in less than an hour."

His boss gives him a look halfway between puzzlement and contempt. "Come on, Kevin! There'll be plenty more soccer games. This is the Sheaffer deal, man!"

This is a ten-second window. How Kevin handles it can make or break a relationship, even a career. What does he do? You could easily make a case that the demand is unfair, yet it is also completely justifiable. It is a moment that gets played out many times in our lives: We are caught between opposing forces, and we stew in the middle.

Kevin performed a Ten-Second Miracle. In the ten seconds after a moment of unfairness, you have a wide-open opportunity to take the whole conversation in a different direction. Kevin changed everything with one simple statement.

He said to Ken, *"I'm really tense, Ken. I'm committed to my kids and I'm committed to you and the company. I don't know what to do."* Then he paused and waited. There was a charged moment of silence, but after a few seconds Ken softened and said, "I see what you mean. Family is important. I like how committed you are to them. Could you take the papers to the game and look them over there? I'll call you on your cell phone when I get to the restaurant, and you can brief me with any problems you see."

Kevin said, "Sure, I can do that easily."

When you are between a rock and a hard place, only a miracle will get you through. Fortunately, once you learn the rules, miracles come quickly.

Notice what Kevin did. Instead of racing to occupy the position of victim—and forcing his boss into the position of persecutor—he told the simple, unarguable truth about real events that were occurring in his body and mind: *I'm really tense, Ken. I don't know what to do.* This move took him out of the victim position and made him Ken's equal. Both of them are in a bind, but Ken had dealt with it by going into a demanding, authoritarian mode and expecting Kevin to cower and acquiesce in response. When you claim victimhood, you give all the power to the other person. All you get out of the deal is the chance to squirrel away some resentment. Kevin, with one statement, made himself Ken's equal, taking himself out of the power disadvantage. It created a miracle.

You might think that Ken would ignore Kevin's statement and steamroller over it. Based on hundreds of real-life situations I've witnessed, I can tell you that this seldom occurs. In actual fact, statements like Kevin's stop people in their tracks. People seldom believe me on this point until they practice the Ten-Second Miracle a few times themselves.

Summary

Now that you have a feel for how people just like you have worked miracles, it's time to learn how to be the miracle worker in your own life. I'm ready to tell you everything I know about creating instant miracles in your life. Speaking as my own best customer, I can say that discovering and putting the Ten-Second Miracle to work has been a magnificent journey of infinite riches.

If you're ready to learn how to do this yourself, turn the page and join me on what could be the most exciting journey of your life.

CREATING RELATIONSHIP MIRACLES

PART ONE

HEART-TO-HEART TALK

Getting What You Need in Relationships:
What You Really Need to Know

An Important Secret

Lean in close for a few moments while I tell you something that I've learned from working with several thousand people on their relationship problems.

> The secret: Commitment is the biggest problem in a relationship, but two other problems always come muddled together with commitment problems. They are so enmeshed that I call them the Three-in-One problem. There is a Ten-Second solution that everybody needs to know and almost nobody does. I want to show you how to solve this problem right now.

Once you take the ten seconds to get the solution, your love life will never be the same.

I commit to helping you solve the Three-in-One problem

in this chapter. Please let me speak to you passionately and frankly. If I come across as blunt, it's because we're dealing with a subject I care about deeply. I have seen a great deal of pain—unnecessary pain—caused by not knowing this secret.

What We Need to Know About Commitment

To begin, I'd like *you* to make a commitment. There is no sense in bothering with this powerful material unless you are willing to make a powerful commitment of your own. Even though you are committed enough to be reading this book, I'd like you to go one step further, into a deeper commitment. I'd like you to make what I call a *whole-body commitment.*

Think of this moment as being like the one in which Columbus got his crew together and said: *We're leaving for a new world. We've got some good evidence that such a world exists—because of stories we've heard—but let's face it, none of us can be sure until we've put our feet on the ground there. I commit myself to doing everything I can to find the new world. I dedicate my life to it. If any of you are not absolutely committed to getting there with me, get off the boat right now. No hard feelings. But if you stay, I'm going to treat you like you're as committed as I am.*

If such an adventure appeals to you, you're ready for . . .

Your Opening Commitment

The commitment: I commit to living in an easeful flow of love and connection, both inside myself and in my key relationships. This is what I really want, and I will stop at nothing to get it.

Pause right now and make that commitment. Make it from the bottom of your heart, in every cell of your body. Make sure this is what you really want. I know it's possible, because I've lived in that flow of love and connection since I discovered what's in this book. I've also cheered as many other people have opened the flow of love and connection. But none of that is going to help you—unless you make a commitment in your bones that it's what you really want. Your commitment initiates the flow of miracles.

The Ten-Second solution to commitment problems begins with pausing to let the commitment settle into your body. Wait until your body says yes! before moving into this big venture. Remove any doubt by making the choice in your body, not just in your mind.

I recommend the following move with any commitment, large or small: *Try the commitment on in your body, and stay with your inner feelings until they say yes.* Many people make mental commitments that have no value because they haven't listened carefully to whether their bodies agree with their minds. Don't make that mistake. To create miracles in your relationships, you'll first need the support of all the cells of your body, those eighteen trillion friends that are standing by to help you. Without them, the road is lonely and the night is long.

Three-in-One

If your body agrees that you are committed, let's move on to the other two problems that are enmeshed with commitment. People have trouble making commitments because they do not make them with their whole beings. They make commitments in their minds and with their mouths but not down in the cells of their bodies. Therefore, they are "out of their bodies" when they make the commitment. Then, when they don't live up to their commitments, they have a built-in excuse: They weren't in their bodies when they made them in the first place!

Join me in my office to see clearly what I mean. The following dialogue is from my first session with a couple in their mid-twenties. Her complaint is that he is vague and indecisive; his complaint is that she's hypercritical, "on my back all the time." After hearing their introductory stories, I begin to pin them both down about the issue of commitment:

ME: Sandra, what do you really, really want from Terry?

SANDRA: What I really want? What I really want is some idea of a wedding date. Our parents have been asking us for a year, and I'm getting tired of saying "I don't know."

ME: Terry, what about it?

TERRY: What about what?

SANDRA: He always does that—pretends he doesn't understand.

ME: What about a wedding date?

TERRY: I just don't know.

ME: Let me be more blunt. Do you want to marry Sandra?

TERRY: Oh, sure.

As he says this, though, he twists sideways in his chair and then rubs the back of his neck.

ME: From your body language, it looks like you have some
    doubts. What are they?

TERRY: I guess I'm really not sure.

ME: Well, tune in and find out—just look and see.

TERRY: How do I do that?

ME: Focus inside for a few seconds until you find out what your
    doubts are.

He spends a few seconds sitting quietly, focusing inwardly.
Sandra is watching intently.

TERRY: *I'm not sure I love her.*

SANDRA (exploding with anger): Terry!

ME: Tell her directly.

TERRY: I'm not sure I love you.

SANDRA: Jesus, Terry, now I find out! How many times have you
    said "I love you" to me? About five thousand?

ME: Both of you take a couple of deep breaths. You may feel
    differently in a moment, but first, just honor the way you
    feel right now. Sandra—embrace your anger. Terry—
    embrace your doubts. Terry, you also look scared to me.
    Check inside and feel if that's true.

TERRY: Well, I've been wanting to say that for a long time, but I
    was afraid she'd get mad, just like she did.

ME: There's something else—I can hear it in your voice.

TERRY: It's not about you, Sandra—*I'm not sure I know what love feels like.* I mean—am I feeling what I'm supposed to be feeling?

ME: Try a Ten-Second experiment. There's a way I've found that will give you a good idea if you really ought to be with someone. Look at Sandra's face—really look at her. *If you were on your deathbed and Sandra's face was the last face you could see before you exited—would this be the face you'd want to be looking at?*

TERRY (nodding emphatically): No question about it.

SANDRA (bursts into tears): Thank you.

ME: Now tune in to your body—what's the feeling that goes along with that?

TERRY: *Kind of a warm spreading glow in my chest.*

ME: A lot of people call that love.

TERRY: I think that's what I'd call it.

Terry learned something we all need to learn: We don't know love—or any other feeling—until we know it in our bodies. When we feel the body sensation of love or commitment or doubt, our minds have something real to hold on to. Without being rooted and grounded in body sensations, our thoughts swing back and forth like monkeys playing on bars.

Before he found love in his body, Terry suffered from the problem that plagues many of us throughout our lives: *We don't know what's true inside ourselves and we don't know how to speak the simple truth to others.* We don't know what's going on in our own bodies! We don't know how to speak the truth! This causes a massive problem: If we don't know ourselves, how are we to know what we want in the first place? If we don't know ourselves, how are we going to know what's causing us to sabotage our commitments? These are the problems that come entangled with our commitment problems.

The payoff for Terry and Sandra was immediate: Those few seconds of contact with his body gave Terry all the certainty he needed. By their second session they had set a date for the wedding. They smoothly navigated the three months leading up to the event with hardly a ruffled sail. They were still doing fine when they moved to the east coast a year later and I lost touch with them.

The Problem That Causes Relationship Distress Also Makes Us Sick and Tired

Before I figured out the Three-in-One problem, my relationships didn't work and I fe¹ tired mc ₒ ₒ ꞔ the time. ᵢ ᵥas sick a lot, too. I would usua. ₔet three ꞏ.ᵤur colds ꞏ yᵣ ᵢr. plus whatever else was going around. Once I figured out The Problem, love started flowing easily in my life. More surprising, I almost never get tired nowadays, even though I'm twenty-five years older. The same is true for illness. I'll occasionally get a flu bug, but often years can go by without a day of sickness. I haven't stayed home from work because of illness in twenty-some years.

What Is "The Problem"?

Put bluntly, The Problem that makes us sick, tired, and hungry for love is this: pretending we're not as we actually are. We perpetrate disease on ourselves every time we create a gap between how we actually are and how we're pretending to be. Into the gap comes a rattle, and the rattle becomes louder the more we pretend it's not there. The solution is: Close the gap and the rattle will stop. You'll hum, and love will flow. Energy and good health will fill the spaces where the rattle used to be.

Pain is created the moment we unconsciously set up an image of *how things are supposed to be* that's in conflict with *how things actually are.* If we notice within ten seconds that we're doing this, we won't feel pain later. For example, you may be angry about something. If you notice it within ten seconds and open up to it, you can use the energy of anger to fuel an action. You can tell somebody what's bothering you or, at the least, acknowledge your anger to yourself. But we think: *I shouldn't be mad* or *It's really nothing* or *It's probably my fault anyway.* By setting up an image of perfection in our minds, we miss the actual perfection of what's going on in our bodies. The anger is real—it's a gift—and it's to be savored and explored rather than made wrong.

The solution hinges entirely on letting go of pretending.

If you watch children pretending not to be upset, you'll see The Problem at a glance. You can see the upset in their bodies, and you can see them stiffening against it by holding their breath and trying to keep their chins from quivering. It's as if they have one foot on the accelerator and one foot on the brakes. The moment they stop pretending they're not upset, the energy of the emotion passes on through and they feel good again.

We do a miniature version of that troublesome move practically every day of our lives. Do it enough and you'll feel sick and tired all the time. Do it in relationships and the love will stop flowing.

Every Ten-Second Miracle Move you'll learn in this book restores flow to yourself and to relationships around you.

We do much of our biggest pretending around sex and anger. In your imagination, revisit the family you were living in when you hit puberty. Picture yourself coming into the living room and announcing, "I'm feeling incredibly sexually aroused today. What should I do about that?"

What would the reaction have been?

Would the people in charge have said, "Great! That's very normal and natural for a person your age. Take a moment to feel it deeply and celebrate it! It's part of the glory of being alive! Make a big distinction between feeling that sensation and expressing it. Feeling it is always a great idea, but expressing it needs to be done with a lot of care. Let's talk about some safe ways and some dangerous ways to express your sexual feelings."

That's not quite the way it would have gone in my family, and maybe not in yours either.

Picture the same sort of conversation with regard to anger. You come into the living room and announce, "I'm incredibly angry right now. What should I do with that?"

Nine times out of ten, the answer is some variation of "You shouldn't feel that way."

By the time we reach adolescence we have become highly skilled at pretending not to be some way we actually are. We've become pros at hiding our hurts, hiding our fears, hiding our wants and needs. When we are hiding who we really are, who we are stays buried inside or reaches the surface in some distorted way. We become silent martyrs or whiny brats. We distract ourselves with food or drink or drugs, all in a vain attempt to keep the pretense going.

When you're angry you're angry. When you're sexy you're sexy. When you're hurt you're hurt.

Do you deserve to be angry right now? It doesn't matter. Is it convenient to be sexy right now? Usually not. Is it logical to be hurt? Often not. None of these things matters. We are whatever we are, and the sickness begins the moment we pretend we're not.

The Problem starts when we pretend to ourselves that we're not the way we are. Then we complicate The Problem by hiding what's real from other people.

That's it.

That's why we get sick and tired and hungry for love. The explanation will never get any more complicated.

I don't think this means we're bad, wrong, or stupid. Some of us may be malicious, but the vast majority of us just fell into the societal trance at an early age and never got nudged awake. We stay entranced until someone cares enough about us to wake us up.

I care about you.

Wake up.

THE MOMENT WE STOP PRETENDING, OUR HEALING BEGINS. After you and I stop pretending, there are many things we can do to feel good, from taking a few deep breaths to getting good medicine to improving our diet. Once you cross the barrier, the world will open up to you magically.

Take a deep breath right now, and approach . . .

The Barrier

There is a barrier that keeps us from making solid commitments and honoring them scrupulously. The barrier is hard to talk about, even among friends. It's defensiveness. It's the outcome of all that pretending we learned to do to survive childhood. We get in the habit of protecting ourselves at an early age by pretending not to be the way we are. After a while we forget we're pretending and it feels real. We think the pretense is who we really are.

Later, when someone comes along and tells us we're being defensive, guess what we do? We get defensive.

I don't believe our defensiveness is usually done for malicious reasons. We're just scared. We're in the dark about what goes on inside ourselves; when we need to explore ourselves deeply, we get scared and defensive.

What Defensiveness Really Is

Defensiveness is the act of hiding ourselves from ourselves. There's only one reason we might want to do that—because we're scared of what we'll find. We also hide ourselves from other people. We do it for the same reason, because we're afraid of what they might think if they knew how we really are on the inside.

Defending is the destructive move that starts the death process in a relationship. Justifying is the move that hastens the death process.

Defending looks like this:

YOU ASK: What are you feeling right now?

YOUR PARTNER REPLIES: Don't you realize *Wheel of Fortune* starts in five minutes? I've got more important things to do than talk about that feeling stuff.

That's defending. Your partner is defending against the learning possibilities that are being offered in the moment.

Justifying often follows a defensive move. It looks like this:

YOUR PARTNER CONTINUES: I've worked my tail off all day and I need a little peace and quiet. We can talk about how I'm feeling later.

Contrast this with a nondefensive reply.

YOU: What are you feeling right now?

YOUR PARTNER (takes several seconds to tune inside): I feel tired and irritable. I'm still feeling leftover frustration from a snafu that happened just before quitting time at work.

Moments like these, taking less than ten seconds, build strength in a relationship. Defending and justifying weaken and eventually kill relationships.

We're all armed with ways to keep ourselves from learning what we need to learn. Some people overeat to drown out their feelings—I've done that one plenty of times. For many years I hid my anger and sadness under a hundred-pound blanket of extra fat. It takes years to store up a hundred pounds of fat, but it's done one bite at a time, to bury one feeling at a time. Every time I sipped a milkshake instead of feeling my sadness, I added another ounce or two to the load. I didn't want to acknowledge how much ancient sorrow I was feeling. I guess it was easier to have people think of me as a fat person than as a sad person. But who was I really fooling?

Some people start arguments with their loved ones to avoid

confronting themselves. I've done my share of that one, too. Kathlyn and I found early in our marriage that we would often have arguments on Friday afternoon, just before a whole weekend of potential intimacy. We figured out that we were afraid of all that open space for intimacy. We didn't know what to do with it. But we did know how to fight. If we could have an argument, we got to stay in the zone of the known. We didn't have to fly out into the risky zone of the unknown.

My biggest self-defense move nowadays is busyness. I keep myself busy so I sometimes don't notice what's going on inside. I don't slow down for the second or two it takes to find out what my body and mind are trying to communicate to me. In the past I used denial—pretending I didn't know—and getting sick to keep the attention away from facing myself.

What should you do with your defensive patterns? The best thing to do is notice them with a clear eye, just as you'd notice what time it is. I invite you to notice any of your defensive patterns that come up as we learn the Ten-Second Miracles. Just notice them and put them on the back burner. Don't take them so seriously, and they'll quit bothering you. When you notice one of your defensive barriers coming up, just think, *There's one of my defensive barriers.* No big deal. Once you learn that knowing yourself feels better than defending yourself, you will automatically gravitate toward the one that feels better.

A Moment of Choice

Commitment gives your choices more power. If you know you are committed to staying sober, for example, you have an easier time choosing to say no when someone offers you a drink. Your commitment gives you a firm place to stand.

The commitment you made a little while ago—to live in an easeful flow of love and connection with yourself and others—gives you a place to stand in the rapidly shifting sands of relationship. Now, if you make a specific choice, your commitment will take on even more power.

The choice: Make a formal and conscious choice between the intention to live in an easeful flow of loving connection and the unconscious intention that usually gets in the way of our creating miracles. The unconscious intention that usually sabotages us is: *I'm more committed to protecting myself than I am to loving and being loved. A less flattering way to say this is that we are more interested in being right than in being loved and loving.*

However we word it, this intention ruins lives, destroys relationships, and even starts wars. Some wise thinkers claim that this intention is wired into our neural machinery. They argue that it's an innate death-and-destroy urge that has built up over thousands of years. Other thinkers, equally wise, say our intention to be right at the expense of being loved is just a bad habit. I say something less philosophical but a lot more practical: Look unflinchingly for ten seconds at your intention to protect yourself and be right, then choose to open yourself to love. I have taken that step myself, and I have invited thousands of others to take it. I recommend that you take it, too. As the philosopher Tasso says, "Any time not spent on love is wasted." I believe that, and I don't want to waste any time. If you feel that way, too, take a deep breath and . . .

Say to yourself and out loud: *I acknowledge the powerful drive in me and other human beings to protect ourselves and be right, and in light of that I choose to make giving and receiving love more important. When faced with the choice between being right and living in the easeful flow of love, I commit to living in the easeful flow of love.*

If you've said that and meant it, you're ready. You are ready to work miracles in the most important area of life. And if you are ready to work miracles, there is one place, and one place only, to start.

THE FIRST MIRACLE: WHAT TO DO

The Ten-Second Inner Shift That Opens the Flow of Miracles

You're only a breath away from the place where miracles are born. I call it the Miracle Zone or the M-Zone. With commitment and a little practice, you can become so comfortable in the M-Zone that you'll be able to live there almost all the time.

To enter the M-Zone, you need to learn one Key Move. It's a simple shift of consciousness, and consciousness is an organic gift you already own. Making the Key Move is like shining a flashlight beam on yourself—a flashlight you already own. With the Key Move, the batteries never run down and the light's always on.

The Key

You already carry the Miracle Zone inside you. You got it free from the factory—there's nothing you need to install. We just need to learn how to turn it on. You also have an organic gift: the key that turns on that power any time you want. In addition to teaching the Key Move to thousands of people, I've been my own best customer. I use this key every day in my life. I've received so many miracles from using the Key Move that I cannot imagine life without it. It would be like driving blindfolded. Speaking as a friend as well as a therapist and teacher, I can tell you there's nothing quite like it.

Listen to Marsha, age 35, as she tells me a wonderful story of how the Key Move stopped an argument in its tracks:

"My husband and I were in the middle of an argument. I know how stupid this sounds, but we were arguing one Saturday morning about whether to buy a sofa or a new bed. The argument had started as soon as our feet hit the floor that morning, and it was getting worse the closer we were to leaving for the furniture store. I stormed into the kitchen to get a cup of tea, and I was so caught up in the heat of the moment that I dropped the cup and it shattered on the floor. My husband had stormed in the other direction toward our bedroom, so he didn't hear the teacup break. I stood there looking at the pieces of the cup, feeling my heart pound, and then the thing you taught me in our first session [the Key Move] popped into my mind. Nothing else was working, so I decided to try it.

"I paused and took a deep breath and felt my body sensations. I felt the layers of anger and anxiety gripping my body. I just felt them, without judging them or doing anything with them. You had said it might take ten seconds, but it didn't take even five. Suddenly all the anger and fear melted and I felt a big open space inside. I could feel how attached I was to being right, and how it really didn't matter. A big smile broke out on my face. Now here's the miracle! At just this moment my husband came into the kitchen with a big smile on *his* face. He saw the broken teacup and looked at me to see if I was all right. There I was, with a big smile on my face, looking at him across a floor with tea and broken china all over it.

"He said, 'I guess this is a good time to tell you I don't care which one we get.'

"I said, 'I don't care either. Let's flip a coin.'

"We both started howling with laughter."

I love these moments; I've felt them often in my relationship with Kathlyn. We'll be stuck in some conflict that an hour later will seem totally ridiculous but at the time feels as though the future of human evolution depended on it. Then one of us lets go and breaks through to the Miracle Zone, that clear space of freedom and ease that's at the center of everything. These are the moments that relationships thrive on: when one person or both make the courageous leap into the zone of the unknown. To stay in the argument is to stay in the zone of the known. We all know how to argue! We've seen a thousand arguments, and most of them ended the same way—with no resolution. But the moment you drop into the Miracle Zone, you open up the possibility of genuine transformation. You break free of the patterns of the past and enter the radiant realm of the miraculous.

On the surface, what Marsha did might seem like a passive move, but it's really anything but passive. In fact, it might be the most active move of all. Just because it takes place inside doesn't make it passive. It takes enormous courage to drop our attachment to being right. When we're attached to being right, we'll sacrifice our happiness and the harmony of the relationship to getting that sofa we want. The Key Move is active because it asks us to put the brakes on the runaway freight train of our thoughts. It's active because it brings the force of years of conditioning to a halt for a moment. It's active because it opens us up to the enormous creative power of the moment.

Let me give you another example, a very practical one that any of you who rush through airports will likely appreciate.

I'm chugging down the concourse at the Denver airport. My flight from L.A. has arrived an hour late, and I'm rushing to make my connection to New York. If I miss this flight, I will have to go into a flurry of rescheduling meetings. I am in a most un-Zen-like state of hurry; I'm very attached to catching that plane, but the clock says I don't have a prayer.

I puff up to the podium, noticing that the staff has already closed the jetway door. An angry fellow in front of me is pounding on the podium and demanding a seat. The agent is patiently explaining that there are no more seats, that the plane is completely full. I look at this unpromising scene, then I see the joke of the whole thing. I realize that I'm so attached to my expectations of how life is supposed to be that I'm not giving it any room to surprise me. So I take my own miracle-medicine: I stop in my tracks and make the Key Move. It takes me a few seconds to breathe through the rattle of anxiety in my body, to feel the free, clear zone deep inside. Soon, though, I'm at ease in the M-Zone. I feel a deep shift of attitude: It truly doesn't matter if I make the flight—I know everything will be fine however it turns out.

Then a remarkable thing happens. The angry fellow storms off up the concourse, threatening lawsuits and vowing that he will never fly this airline again. I move to the front spot, where the harried clerk is bent over his computer. Just then a flight attendant rushes up and tells the clerk that there's been a miscount. One seat remains. I see the clerk glance up the concourse toward the receding back of the man who was hassling him. I see a Cheshire-cat smile of satisfaction playing around the clerk's mouth as he makes a decision. He looks at me and asks, "Going to New York?" It turns out the one remaining seat is in first class, and moments later I'm settling into my big, comfy seat, sipping champagne, and writing a note of appreciation to the airline about the exemplary clerk in its employ.

These moments at first may seem rare and unpredictable, but they can be cultivated. It just takes practice. With a little practice you'll be able to make your Miracle Moves in much less than ten seconds—more like the time it takes to draw a relaxed breath. The road to miracles begins with learning a rule we should have learned in kindergarten and practiced every day thereafter. We didn't, though, so let's learn it now.

The First Miracle Rule

We all have the Miracle Zone inside us. It's free and clear and open to infinite possibility. You can enter the M-Zone many ways, but the easiest place to enter is through body sensation, no matter how pleasant or unpleasant. The Rule: *When you rest pure, nonjudgmental attention for ten seconds on any tension or feeling in your body, the tension or feeling will melt into flowing sensation, then to spacious openness.* The Miracle Zone is that feeling of spacious openness. Miracles spontaneously happen around anyone who's occupying that zone of spacious openness. From within the zone you can consciously create miracles of your own design.

The good news is this: You can enter the Miracle Zone through tight shoulders or a wave of heartache. All you do is rest nonjudgmental attention on the sensation for ten seconds. You can enter through a shiver of fear and within ten seconds feel it turn into pleasurable waves of excitement. You can enter through a tight fist of anger and within ten seconds feel a warm rush of gratitude. The Miracle Zone is always there and waiting for you, even if you have been on a downward spiral for months or years.

The Key Move

The easiest way to start working miracles is to learn to rest your attention for ten seconds on places in your body. Ten seconds is not an arbitrary number: My clients revealed it to me. Twenty-some years of working with people showed me that ten seconds was the average time they took to access the M-Zone. It might take you two seconds or twelve seconds—it's really not important how long it takes. It's only important that you give it the time it takes for you. I predict, though, that by the end of this section you will come to realize that ten seconds is an eternity. It's plenty of time to make the important shifts that will change your relationship life.

Honoring Your Key Body Sensation

To help you become your own miracle worker, I'm going to ask you to become highly skilled at doing something completely radical, something almost no one knows how to do well. I'm going to ask you to *honor* something that most people ignore or dishonor all their lives. Not only will I ask you to do this odd thing, but I will make you a radical promise. If you learn to do it well, you will feel more love and happiness than you ever imagined.

If you learn to rest your consciousness on certain sensations that occur organically in your body, you'll not only learn to create miracles in your love life, you'll get in touch with an organic sense of divinity. Again, I'm not saying this to prove some theory: My clients revealed it to me. Time and again, when they learned to do the Key Move, they told me that it helped them make powerful shifts in their relationships, and it enabled them to feel a sense of divinity. No matter what religion they came from, they could feel the sense of organic divinity inside. That wasn't why I was asking them to do the Key Move, but it turned out to be a wonderful side effect. I'm all for things that make us feel more divine. The more divine we feel, the better we treat one another.

You enter the Miracle Zone when you rest your awareness on the reality of your body sensations. The act of focusing consciousness on it calls forth the consciousness behind and around it. Consciousness comes forth to meet consciousness, and from that union the miracle is born. Usually the constriction loosens within seconds, and you begin to feel the flow of good feeling again. You also liberate the frozen, trapped energy of the constriction so that you can turn it into action.

My own life changed dramatically when I learned to honor my Key Sensation, the very one I want you to learn to honor. Honoring it allowed me to lose a great deal of weight, kick a life-threatening addiction, regain my health, and create my happy marriage of nearly two decades. Long before I began

using the phrase *Ten-Second Miracle,* just such a miracle
moment started me on my path to wholeness. In 1968 a man
named George had the courage to confront me about my
destructive behavior, and I believe the moment saved my life.
He pointed out that I was a hundred pounds overweight,
smoked like a chimney, and was in a relationship that I complained about constantly. At first, I was furious at him. I later
found that many people react with anger when the obvious is
called to their attention. George asked: "Why are you so bent
on killing yourself? You have so much potential. Why are you
trying to destroy it?"

I spent two weeks avoiding his question by making him
wrong and overeating and getting sick with a cold. But then,
life caught up with me. I stopped my abuse of myself for a
moment one day and looked unflinchingly at his question. I
took the Ten-Second path: I simply felt my feelings of rage
and helplessness and despair. And down in the middle of all
those feelings, I found the clear space. I realized I was killing
myself in exactly the same way my father had killed himself.
He had died at age 32—grossly obese, in a difficult relationship, and smoking two packs of unfiltered Camels a day. He
had died with all his potential fully intact. ·

My ten seconds of being with myself showed me that I was
replaying his sad life in uncanny detail. I believe that those
ten seconds of confrontation with myself enabled me to
break free. During the hard work to come, I had those ten seconds of clarity to refer back to. And I had to refer to them
often, because it takes a lot of work to lose a hundred pounds,
stop smoking, and get out of a bad relationship in one year.
But I did it, and I'm here today because I did.

I still use the Key Move every day of my life. I've also had the pride and pleasure of being with thousands of people as they changed their lives by learning to make their Key Moves. That's why I can say with confidence: Your life will change for the better the moment you learn to do this simple thing.

Over the years, considerable scientific data have been collected about the power of the Miracle Moves you'll learn in this book. Let me give you an example of what I mean. The accompanying chart shows the neck and shoulder tension of a woman as she applies the Key Move you're about to learn. The machine, called an EMG, measures tension. In this chart, you can see how the tension drops when she does the Key Move.

Why would a simple shift of consciousness produce this kind of immediate physical result?

It works because of another part of the First Miracle Rule:

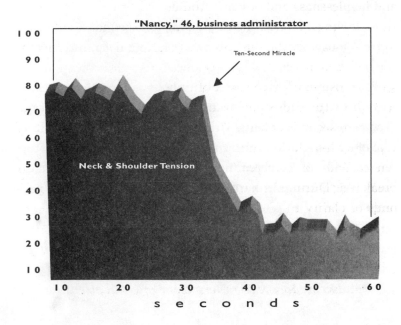

A flow toward happiness and harmony begins when we rest nonjudgmental attention on anything real and unarguably true inside ourselves. The Key Move is a highly specific way of resting attention on something very real: our core body sensations. The woman's neck and shoulders relaxed because she embraced something true and real—and all it took was a ten-second shift of attention.

Now, back to the Key Move.

My colleagues and I call it a key because it always unlocks the door to a rich treasure trove of life-changing knowledge. Everyone can learn to do it, usually within a few run-throughs. And since the run-throughs take only ten seconds, it is extremely efficient.

And now, if you are ready, let's take ten seconds and do it.

The Instructions

First, get a body-sense of how long ten seconds is. Count it off on your watch right now while taking deep, full breaths in and out.

For most people, ten seconds is about as long as it takes for two or three deep, slow breaths in and out. During all of our Ten-Second experiments—whenever you see the graphic of the clock—use two or three slow, deep breaths as your "stopwatch." Using your breath rather than looking at your watch will free up more of your attention to focus on the experiment.

Now that you have a body-sense of what ten seconds feels like, it's time to learn the Key Move.

For ten seconds, rest your nonjudgmental attention on

*your inner sensations from your head down through your
stomach. Focus on all those areas as a whole, as if you're
taking a ten-second movie of them.*

*Feel your inner sensations from your head down
through your stomach as you take two or three deep, slow
breaths, starting now.*

*If your mind wandered before you got through two or
three breaths, that's natural and normal. Just go back and
do it again until you can keep your attention on your
sensations for two or three full breaths in and out.*

A Key Question

*Now I want to ask you a question about your
experience during those ten seconds. There are no right or
wrong answers to the question. It's only for your benefit,
so be honest with yourself.*

*When you felt your sensations from your head down
through your stomach, did the sensations, taken as a
whole, feel more like this:*

Constricted . . . a little "off" . . . not flowing easefully?
Or more like this:
Spacious . . . open . . . flowing easefully?

If you get an immediate answer, fine. If you don't, that's
fine too. About half the people I work with can tell right
away whether they feel the contracted-constricted-uneasy
sensations or the open-spacious-easy ones. The other half
need to do the Ten-Second experiment again before they can

tell for sure.

Since this experiment is so important, I want you to do it again with a slight change of instructions. More than half the people I work with have difficulty focusing for the full ten seconds. This doesn't mean there's something wrong with you—after all, what I'm asking you to do is probably not something you practice very much.

Let me show you a trick I teach that often helps people get more in touch with their sensations. Some of us, myself included, find that closing the eyes helps us feel the sensations more clearly. When the eyes are open, more than 50 percent of our attention is used visually. Closing the eyes frees up that attention to be focused on our body sensations.

You be the judge of whether it helps. Of course, if you are in a situation where it would cause problems to close your eyes, don't close them.

Let's do the experiment again, using the new instructions. Here's the way I say it:

> *Close your eyes and focus your nonjudgmental attention on your body sensations, from your head down through your stomach.*
> *Taken as a whole, were your sensations more like this:*
> Constricted . . . a little "off" . . . not flowing easefully?
> *Or more like this:*
> Spacious . . . open . . . flowing easefully?

By now you probably have a sense of whether you are feeling flow or constriction. So that we can put this information to use, let's find out exactly what it is you're feeling inside.

What Is the Key Sensation?

The Key Sensation—the "snapshot" you just took—is the sum of the sensations in *three core zones* of your body:

- Your upper back, neck, and shoulders.

- Your throat and chest.

- Your stomach and abdomen.

These zones have a very specific way of communicating with you: They talk to you through the *sensations* you feel in them. It has taken millions of years of evolution to develop the language of these sensations. They're worth paying attention to.

The three zones signal you with specific sensations—that's their language. You're already skilled at listening to the sensations from some of your zones. For example, your bladder has evolved an unmistakable way of telling you when it's time to go to the bathroom. Your three core zones have their language, too, and the information is just as important. It's just that no one teaches us how to listen to it. By the time you got to kindergarten, you could speak "bladder language" pretty well, and now you're completely fluent. We need to become as fluent with the other zones.

You might wonder why we're not considering the sensations from your sexual zone. Practically speaking, our sexual sensations are usually pretty clear to us by the time we reach adulthood. I've found relatively few people who couldn't decipher whether or not they were sexually aroused (if they were willing to be honest about it!). For now, we will work with the zones that cause the most difficulties in everyday life.

I mentioned that the Key Sensation is a snapshot of three zones, taken as a whole. If your snapshot told you that you are feeling uneasy, tight, or slightly "off," that's very useful information. In fact, consider it good news. It's telling you something that could change your life and possibly save it. I'm not exaggerating: I've seen it save many people's lives.

The Key Sensation is an inner signal system. Learn to notice it, and you will have a navigational instrument of exceptional power. The uneasy/constricted/"off" sensation tells you when you need to look closely at something important that's going on, something you may not be paying attention to. The easy/flowing/open sensation tells you when you are on the right track in life—it's saying, Keep on doing what you're doing.

Your Key Sensation Is Always There for You

Your Key Sensation is always ready and waiting to serve you. Listen to this description from a woman who learned it during a workshop at my institute and put it to work that evening:

"I drove home from the workshop feeling very excited yet very calm at the same time. I got out of the car and went toward my front door. As I touched the doorknob, I realized I was holding my breath and feeling slightly constricted in my chest and stomach. I paused for a moment, with my hand on the doorknob, and scanned my body sensations. Suddenly it was clear to me: I was scared and sad. I took a deep breath and got my inner flow going again. I let myself into the house and stood there inside the doorway for a few moments, just breathing. A few seconds later I realized that I was hurt about an argument with my son before breakfast. He wanted to drop out of college for a term and travel on the west coast. I didn't want him to do it. Just then, he came out of his bedroom and said 'Hi.' We sat down in the kitchen and talked it over. We got about five minutes into the argument and had a huge blowup. I had to walk around the block and do the Key Move a few more times until I felt relaxed inside. After a few more go-rounds, we reached a compromise. He would finish out the year, then go traveling in the summer, and if he still didn't want to go back, he would work and travel on into the fall."

This is a perfect example of how the First Miracle can open an inner flow that leads to connection. The art of relationships is noticing when the connection has been broken and knowing what to do to reopen it. First the flow must be opened inside ourselves; then we can take on the more complicated task of opening it with others. Fortunately, once you know what to look for in yourself, you can tell in a split second when you're out of connection.

More About the Key Sensation

The uneasy/constricted part of the Key Sensation can also be thought of as a *diffuse sensation of longing.* There is a sharper sensation of longing, which most people feel in the chest (we'll learn more about that later), but the Key Sensation is vaguer and more spread out. It's not a longing for a certain person; it's a longing for union with yourself. The woman in the example above longed for connection with her own core feelings, and she also longed for connection with her son. Her body sensations were there to remind her to restore connection with herself and her son.

When we're out of touch with ourselves, we yearn to return to our deep connection with all our body sensations. For example, if you ignore the sensations flowing from the zone of your body that's telling you when you're angry, your body will try to get your attention with the sensations of constriction and ill-ease that we're calling the Key Sensation. If you overlook the Key Sensation long enough, your body responds with an even stronger message, dis-ease. Then we're forced to pay attention the hard way. I want you to get your messages the easy way. Learn to slow down and notice the sign that says SPEED BUMP AHEAD, rather than shutting your eyes and learning about it the hard way.

The uneasy/constricted part of the Key Sensation is also a longing for completion. When something triggers your anger or your fear, for example, your body will live in a state of incom-pletion until you consciously greet those feelings. In this book you will learn to say hello to them within ten seconds. Our research shows that this is your window of greatest opportunity to handle them effectively. If you don't acknowledge them, your body will yearn for completion until you do. The unpleasant part of the Key Sensation is your body's yearning for completion.

The open/spacious/flowing part of the Key Sensation occurs when we are in harmony with ourselves and other people. We feel open and flowing when we are in tune with our own feelings and experiencing a sense of connection with others. That's when life is working. That's when we should keep on doing whatever we're doing, and look for ways to do it more.

The Cost of Ignoring Key Sensations

We pay dearly for our lack of education in listening to our bodies. It costs us health, happiness, and love. *The failure to notice Key Sensations keeps us from taking correct actions in the most important areas of our lives.* It's like driving a car: If you and I are driving along and hear an unusual knocking coming from the engine, the best move is to pay close attention to it. Then, we need to take an action that restores the healthy hum to our ride. What we must not do is turn up the radio to get rid of the knocking in the engine! Yet that's what society, mainly the advertising industry, trains us to do.

By the time we trek off to school for the first time, we've already been bombarded with thousands of ads that tell us:

If you're feeling low, perk yourself up with a Pepsi or a Twinkie.

If you want camaraderie, crack open a beer with your buddies.

If you want to be a manly man, smoke Marlboros; if you want to be a powerful career woman, grip a briefcase in one hand and a Virginia Slim in the other.

At the "first sign of impending headache," reach for your favorite pain reliever.

After being inundated with this kind of advice for a few years, we start misinterpreting our Key Sensation. We take it as a sign that the level of nicotine, sugar, or beer in our blood is dropping to a dangerous low. We tear open a cellophane bag when we should be opening the windows of perception.

Now that you know what the problem is and that we all have it in one form or another, what do we do about it?

The Next Step

Now that you've done the Key Sensation experiment, I want to go to the next step. Keep in mind, though, that noticing the Key Sensation, *especially when it shifts from one type to the other* (for example, from "easefully flowing" to "uneasy"), is the foundation of the Ten-Second Miracle that will change your life.

Putting the Key Sensation to Work

As your skill in noticing the Key Sensation grows, you will be able to do the quick scan of head-to-waist sensations in a split second rather than in ten seconds. You will develop an ability to know immediately whether you are feeling . . .

Uneasy OR Easeful,

Spacious OR Contracted,

Open OR Constricted.

It becomes easy with practice. Your body organically wants you to know these things, so it will reward you immensely when you begin to pay attention. The forces of society—advertising, authoritarian religion, repressive schooling—want you to ignore your body sensations. With practice, though, you can use the Key Sensation every moment of your life.

Here is another example, given to me by an executive at an advertising agency:

"I was in the photocopy room one day when a colleague came in. We had a brief chat about a presentation, then I went back to my office. I noticed that I had shifted into an uneasy sensation. I was definitely not feeling 'in the flow' anymore.

"What happened?

"I tuned in to my body sensations for a moment: There was a tight, pulling sensation between my shoulder blades, and my neck was getting stiff. I realized I was angry. Quickly I scanned back over the interaction in the copy room. My colleague had made a sarcastic remark about one of my presentations, but I'd let it go by without saying anything. The irritation was still stuck in my body—probably because I hadn't said anything. I picked up the phone and called him. 'Bart, when you said that thing about my slides being upside down in the machine during the Osgood presentation, I felt angry but I didn't say anything. When I got back to my office, I noticed my shoulders and neck were tight. I wanted to tell you so I didn't carry it around all day.' He seemed kind of stunned and didn't say much, but my shoulders and neck relaxed right away. Later he came by my office and told me he had made the sarcastic remark because he was jealous of my ability to speak in public."

Meet Your Oldest Friend

The great value of the Ten-Second Miracle is that you can do something on the spot that restores the flow of ease. But you won't be able to do it without the information from your million-year-old body. The human body and its sensations have been around much longer than our thinking brain. The human body has survived and prospered by being sensitive to

the Key Sensation. Once you become skilled at feeling its signals, I predict that you'll come to think of your body and its
sensations as your Oldest Friend.

It's been only fairly recently that we've drowned out the
signals from our Oldest Friend. We've lost touch with our
Friend owing to lack of education, the visual and auditory
noise of modern life, and the relentless persuasions of the
advertising industry and its trance-meisters. We miss our
Friend sorely . . . with the accent on *sore*. Missing the signals
from our Oldest Friend will create pain and disease faster
than the bugs and germs we fear so much.

At every moment, though, we're only seconds away from
embracing our Oldest Friend. Now that you've met, let's get
to know your Friend more intimately.

What does the Key Sensation unlock?

We'll use the Key Sensation all by itself for making Miracle Moves, and we'll also use it for opening the door to four
other life-changing sensations. These are all gifts from your
million-year-old Friend.

Three Zones, Three Specific Sensations

When you notice the Key Sensation, you can quickly shine
the flashlight of your awareness on three specific places. Each
of them will give you essential information.

As we go into this powerful work, you can expect that
your mind will wander quite a bit. *The reason is that disso-
ciation—spacing out—is one of the four main results of any
painful life situation*, whether it's emotional trauma or a
physical accident. When we have a trauma, we *tense up, rev*

up, *freeze up*, or *space out*. Later, when we go back to put our attention on some wounded place in ourselves, our minds will naturally space out again to keep us from going through that door again. The trick is to notice when you space out and bring your attention right back again.

Zone One

Right now, rest your nonjudgmental attention on your upper back. For ten full seconds—the time it takes for two to three deep breaths—feel the sensations between your shoulder blades, then move your awareness up into your neck and shoulders and on into your jaws.
Are these areas . . .
Tight and uneaseful?
OR
Relaxed and easeful?
Just notice how you feel, and let's move on to . . .

Zone Two

For ten full seconds, rest your nonjudgmental attention on the sensations inside your throat and chest.
Is your throat . . .
Open and easeful?
OR
Constricted?
Are your chest sensations more like this:
Tight . . . heavy . . . not full breaths?
OR

Open . . . light . . . breathing freely?

Take note of the sensations you feel, and let's move on to Zone Three.

Zone Three

For ten full seconds, feel the sensations inside your stomach area . . . from the bottom of your heart down to beneath your navel.
Are your sensations more like this:
Uneasy . . . speedy . . . "butterflies" . . . queasy . . . tight?
OR
Pleasant . . . flowing . . . easy . . . relaxed?

What the Signals Are Saying

What are these body sensations trying to tell you? Remember, they are *not* signals from your socialized mind—your sensations are signals directly from your mammalian nervous system, which was here long before our modern minds developed. Even though your socialized mind might argue with your body, *your body is always right*. It cannot lie. It's always giving us the straight stuff—it's up to us to learn what to do with the information.

Let me give you a personal example of how to use the straight stuff that comes from paying attention to your Key Sensation.

Opening to My Key Sensation

As I scan my body right now, I feel open and easyfully flowing execpt for the area of my high chest and throat. There's a cloudy sensation there, a feeling of slight constriction. I pause and rest my attention on it for ten seconds.

I realize I feel sad. As I feel the sensations of the sadness, a picture of my granddaughter, Elsie, comes into my mind. I realize I'm sad and missing her. It has taken me only a few seconds to tune in to that feeling, but as I tune in to it I realize it's been in the background all day. I just hadn't listened to it! Just noticing it, I feel the sensations in my throat beginning to loosen and flow with ease. I think of an action I could take. The idea comes to me: Just send her my love and blessings through the airwaves. I close my eyes, picture her beautiful face, and send her a telepathic blessing. I pick up the phone and, finding nobody home, leave a message for her and her parents.

I take a quick snapshot of my Key Sensation. From head through belly, I feel a delicious melting sensation of flowing ease.

That's how simple it is. In that spirit of ease, let's go more deeply into the language spoken by our sensations.

Each Zone Has a Feeling and a Need

Zone One

Zone One—your upper back, neck, and jaws—tightens when you're angry. If you hide or ignore the anger signals, Zone One will escalate into signals of soreness and pain. When you're angry, *you need to become equal.* The anger will keep recycling until you get into an equal relationship with whatever is triggering your anger. Often, *a fundamental unfairness* is driving your anger, and this unfairness must be rectified. I'll show you how to do this (in less than ten seconds) in a later section, but for now, just know that tension in Zone One is giving you incredibly useful information about the feeling of anger and what you need to resolve it.

What causes the sensations of Zone One to fire off? One of the main things is trespass.

Trespass occurs when we feel intruded or encroached upon. We register anger when our physical or moral boundaries are transgressed. First, the upper back starts tightening. This is the situation in which a cat's or dog's hackles start rising, and we've got the same wiring. Watch a dog when an intruder comes up the driveway. The hair along its upper spine will rise and the dog will snarl and bark. There is no doubt that the dog is angry, and no doubt that the trigger is trespass. Contrast this with the same dog's reaction when its owner comes home and finds that the dog has tipped over and looted the garbage can. The dog will bow its head and shrink. There's no doubt here, either. The dog is scared of its owner's reaction, afraid that it will be struck or scolded. The dog's body is not registering trespass—it's registering threat, which triggers fear. We'll get to that one in a moment.

A common form of trespass, one that occurs often in our world, is unfairness. When you see someone taking advantage of another person, purely because one has more power than the other, that's unfairness. It makes our hackles rise, and there is often not much we can do about it. Not until the Ten-Second Miracle came along, anyway.

Dealing with Trespass

If we don't deal with trespass quickly and effectively, the

tightening spreads up into neck, shoulders, and jaws. Ignore those sensations and you'll often have a headache or back pain a little while later. Respond to the sensations correctly and you'll feel expansion and relaxation in your back and neck.

The correct response to trespass—what you need in that kind of situation—is *to become equals* with the other person or persons. As I said, we'll discuss later just how to do that, and when we finish, you'll have an amazing new way to deal with something that creates havoc in life if we don't know how to handle it.

Something to Think About

Think about how often in a given day the average person encounters a situation in which his or her physical or moral boundaries are violated. Think about how little training any of us gets in handling these moments with techniques like the Ten-Second Miracle Moves you are learning. Think about how many people in the United States have chronic headaches (twenty-five million or so) and chronic back pain (more than seventy million).

It's really worth becoming a keen observer of that little sensation in your upper back that says you're angry.

Zone Two

Your throat and chest tighten to tell you that you're feeling sadness or longing. The constriction can range from a mild sense of thickening when your feelings are hurt, to a full-fledged lump in the throat when you contemplate a profound loss. Many people think that crying is the signal of sadness, but before your eyes shed tears, you'll notice the gathering of constriction in your throat.

The trigger for sadness is *loss*. When you're sad, your body is feeling the loss of something important to it. The message is: Slow down and pay attention . . . there's something that needs to be said or some sound that needs to come out of your throat. It could be a sob or a howl or words such as "I don't want you to leave." The constriction is reminding you to say something that restores the flow of ease to your throat.

We experience many losses in daily life, and many more powerful ones over a lifetime. The loss of a loved one, through death or disconnection, is the most profound loss we usually experience. But there are others that greatly affect us:

A broken promise about something heartful.

Loss of respect for someone we love.

Loss of a possible source of creative fulfillment (the critics pan your play; you break an ankle and can't ski).

Loss of approval of someone who matters to us.

All these losses, and more, pass through our lives more often than we probably realize. Your body and mine register these losses, whether or not our minds acknowledge them. It's not important to actually sob or howl on the spot—you might be in a meeting or at the movies when you feel the urge. But you need to acknowledge the urge, even if you don't express it, so that you can keep open the flow of energy in your throat.

What we need when we're feeling sad is *to resonate with the reality of the loss* until we feel a body-release of acceptance. When we won't allow our bodies to resonate with reality, we

feel a despairing sadness all the time. The sadness will release
as we face the reality squarely and feel in harmony with it.

What we need when we're feeling longing is *to resonate
with the feeling until we know what we're really longing for.*

A woman in my office tells me about an immense pressure
on her chest. It has been there since her husband died two
years ago. Now she's worried about her health, and rightfully so.
When we carry sadness for a long time, it begins to weigh down
upon our organs and immune system as well as our hearts.

I invite her to do the Key Move. She rests her consciousness
on the pressure for a few seconds, then slips off into a fit of
coughing. We return to the pressure. Again she slips off after a
few seconds—she finds herself holding her breath and thinking
about something unrelated. We return to the Key Move. Finally,
she stays with the sensation steadily for a full three breaths.

"I haven't been able to accept that I lost my best friend," she
says suddenly. I wait for a moment, then ask if there's anything
else. She nods: "I'm sure I'm never going to have another friend
as long as I live." As she says this, she begins to cry and continues for several minutes. "You really long for that connection you
had," I say. She nods through her tears. After a minute or so, her
tears stop and she takes a deep breath. When she does the Key
Move again, the pressure has released.

Let's look carefully at what happened. She had given up
("I'm never going to have another friend . . . ") because she had
not fully accepted and embraced the sadness. When she fully
felt the sadness, the pressure began to melt. I believe that the
pressure would have stayed until she resonated with the reality of the loss, no matter how long it took to face it. With

guidance, though, it took only ten seconds, once she could keep her consciousness with it long enough.

Now let's move on to the other core feeling of Zone Two. *That closed-fist sensation in your chest is the sensation of longing.* The open-flowing sensation in your chest is when your longing is fulfilled. Longing is when we are not in union with our heart's desire. It can be a person we long for, or it can be a state of consciousness, such as connection with God. Most of us also long for the fulfillment of our creative destiny—to write the book or build the house or cook the soup that lives within us as potential. Since we long for so much and have so little time to complete our destinies, many of us live in the grip of constant longing.

When we're in union with what we long for—entwined in the arms of our beloved or writing a poem as the dawn breaks— the grip of longing releases and the flow of love courses through us. When the grip of the fist relaxes, we are in heaven. When it tightens to a white-knuckle clench, we're in hell.

When you're feeling longing, you need to take actions toward union. Exactly how to do that will be discussed in the section on the Second Miracle.

Zone Three

The speedy, queasy sensation in your stomach lets you know you're scared. The sensations can be as fluttery as butterflies or as solid as a block of ice. Fear gears the body up for action, giving you that speedy feeling. Your stomach feels fluttery and queasy because your digestion has slammed to a halt. Your Oldest Friend learned long ago that it is not possible to digest food and deal with threats and predators at the same time. Your Friend puts the brakes on digestion when you're scared.

The old fears were all physical threats. Our ancestors who lived in trees developed a great fear of falling, and you can feel that fear still living in your body today. They were also stalked by predators much larger than they. They survived only through good luck and their skill at throwing rocks and sharp sticks. Today, though, most of our threats do not have fangs and claws. The things we fear today are mostly social: criticism, humiliation, embarrassment, rejection. Often, the modern fears are more intense than anything on the physical level. I recall working with a man who had led dozens of missions through enemy fire. He told me that nothing he'd faced in war was as scary as thinking of his wife's wrath when he contemplated confessing an affair.

There's something extremely ironic about a decorated soldier—one who has personally killed people—cowering in fear about saying a simple sentence to his wife. Why could he kill people but not bring himself to say "I'm cheating"? The reason gets to the heart of what makes us scared. Killing an enemy in war does not present a contradiction. The contradiction is resolved for the soldier because the killing is done for country, God, home, and flag. But the affair is a different matter. Here, my client could not face the contradictions that his behavior had brought up:

How could I, who vote Republican and passionately preach family values, have done something that's caused me to shrink in shame from my family?

How could I, who punish my children when *they* lie, be living a lie myself?

How can I simultaneously want my stable life with my won-

derful Sunday-school-teacher wife and yet get so much exhilaration from sex with a 27-year-old cocktail waitress with a tat-
too that says "Let's Jam"?

It's a contradiction.

Fear shimmers in our bodies when we cannot embody a
contradiction. The biggest modern fears—the ones that make
us not only shimmer but shake and numb ourselves—come
from huge contradictions we cannot possibly resolve:

> How can I, who can contemplate infinity, also live in a finite
> body that, by all the evidence, is going to die?
>
> How can someone who loves me and takes me to play in the
> park also get drunk and beat me up?
>
> How can God, portrayed as benign and omnipotent, allow
> such suffering to go on?
>
> How can someone I love so deeply not love me in return?

We live in the grip of fear until we can make room in our
bodies for such contradictions. When we can't make the
room, our bodies signal us by going into overdrive. Everything speeds up slightly or mightily, and we begin to digest
ourselves instead of our food.

The correct response to fear is to make yourself safe. You
do this by removing the threat, resolving the contradiction,
or making yourself a safety zone. I'll have more to say about
this later.

Summarizing the Three Zones

When your back, neck, and shoulders get tight, your body

is telling you you're angry. Never mind whether your mind thinks it's appropriate to be angry! Maybe later you can get your mind to tell your body some bit of wisdom that will keep it from getting angry next time. But right now your neck and back and shoulders are the way they are. You need to get equal.

When your throat is constricted, you're sad. You've experienced a loss. You need to get into harmony with the way things are. Harmonizing with reality will release the energy required to move you forward.

When your chest is tense, you're longing for something. You need to take actions that bring you into union with what you're longing for.

When you're feeling fluttery, racy, and queasy, you're scared. There's a threat—sometimes physical, usually not. When you feel a threat, you're worried that you're going to be hurt. You need to remove the threat, or resolve the contradiction on which the fear is based, or create a zone of safety around you. None of these things is hard to do—they can all be done in ten seconds or less. The hard part is getting your mind to focus long enough to do them. The territory is strange and you're moving fast: That's why it's good to have a guidebook in your hand.

Each of these core sensations is telling you that *a specific action needs to be taken.* The actions are all simple and clear, and we should have learned them in kindergarten. We didn't, though, so we're going to work on them in the next chapter. Before we move on, let's take one more quick trip through the Key Move. This time we'll add a final key instruction. You'll be using the full Key Move often in our work together, so let's spend another minute . . .

Putting It All Together

Now we will put one final touch on your Key Move. I want you to rest your consciousness on your sensations long enough to feel "the blossoming of flow," as one of my clients so beautifully named it. If you give your full, innocent attention to any sensation, you will feel a sweet, flowing sensation begin in and around the area. It will actually feel like something pleasant has "blossomed" there. This is a good sign—it lets you know you are entering the Miracle Zone.

Ready? Let's go . . .

Take your head-to-stomach "sensation snapshot" and notice whether your overall feeling is easefully flowing or not. If you're flowing easefully, keep on doing what you're doing. If not, rest your nonjudgmental attention on your core zones—upper back and neck, throat and chest, stomach—for ten seconds, as if "listening" to them with your inner awareness. Feel them and listen to them steadily, generously, and intently for ten full seconds. As you scan the three core zones—upper back, throat, chest, stomach—feel where the flow is most blocked. Rest your attention on the most-blocked zone first, then move on to others that feel blocked. Rest your attention on the blocked sensations long enough to feel a flowing sensation or spacious openness around and behind the blocked sensations. It usually takes about ten seconds for most people to feel the flowing or spacious sensation around and behind the blocked sensations. Do your best to be generous with yourself . . . stay with the sensations until you feel space and flow around and behind them.

Your first Miracle Move is resting your attention on the core zones for a few seconds—without taking any other action. It's often the only thing you need to do. In some situations, you need to combine the Key Move with the Key Relationship Move, which we will explore in the section on the Second Miracle. Often, however, the Key Move shifts you into miracle mode all by itself. Despite its simplicity, the Key Move has awesome power. Let me explain why.

Why the Key Move Produces Miracles

Our problems begin the moment we unground ourselves by separating our minds from our bodies. Our problems move toward resolution the moment we reground ourselves in reality by bringing our minds into harmony with our bodies. Your organic body sensations are the best place to do this. It's hard to argue with your body sensations. You may not know whether you're angry or sad, but you can usually tell if your stomach feels tight or not. Once you put your attention on the unarguable, you are in harmony with yourself.

We are brainwashed early and often to leave behind the reality of our body sensations. The message is drummed into us day after day: Don't feel what you feel . . . don't want what you want. As a result, we use our powerful minds to distance ourselves from our bodies. Often, the more powerful our minds are, the greater the gap is between mind and body. I've had the opportunity to work with celebrated writers and thinkers, and some of them have been pathetically out of touch with their bodies. Of course, the greater the gap between mind and body, the more dramatic is the moment of reunion. I've enjoyed many wonderful reunion moments (such as watching a smile break out on the face of a famous relationship expert when he was finally able to *feel* his feelings instead of merely philosophize about them).

Once we abandon the reality of our feelings and sensations, we get lost in the labyrinths and cul-de-sacs of our beliefs, opinions, and self-deceptions. The quick way to reground ourselves in reality is to focus nonjudgmentally on our body sensations. It brings us home.

Shifting our awareness into the reality of our feelings and sensations puts us squarely in harmony with *what actually is*. When you are in touch with what is, you have a gift beyond price: You are in harmony with the source of creation in the universe. You are in exactly the same position as the oak tree and the ocean wave and the movement of the planets. Most people don't bother to argue with ocean waves. Since the Renaissance, most people don't argue with the movement of the planets. Most people just stand back and appreciate the power of forces of nature. The moment you ground yourself in the reality of your body sensations, you align yourself with those forces.

Our first big mistake is to argue with *what is* inside ourselves. Our bodies are screaming "you're angry" and our minds are busily saying "shut up." Our bodies are saying "I'm hurt" and our minds are saying "You have no right to be." It's as if we are driving with one foot on the accelerator and another on the brakes. No wonder we squeal, wear out, and break down.

Our second big mistake is arguing with *what is* in other people. They're screaming "I'm hurt"—silently or in words—and we are saying "You have no right to be." Inside us or in a relationship, the argument with reality causes pain. Just as our ears hurt when we hear discordant music, our bodies hurt when we are in disharmony with ourselves or others. The Key Move resolves the problem: The moment you rest your consciousness on the reality of your sensations, you heal the hurts and harmonize yourself. Life flows, inside and outside, and the world is right again.

Let me share one more powerful example with you, from a young woman who had recently taken a one-week class at my institute:

"I was having a busy and productive day at work when about 11:30 I noticed a shift in my body, a sense of uneasiness. It occurred to me that I could use the Ten-Second Miracle I'd learned in the class. As I scanned my body I noticed an enormous amount of tension in my nose and down through my chest. As soon as I tuned in to this sensation, I realized I'd actually been feeling it for a couple of months. I don't know why I didn't really pay attention to it until now.

"I went into an empty room at work and put my attention on the sensation for ten seconds. Suddenly a memory flashed into my mind that this had something to do with 'not being a crybaby' when I was a kid. When I was little I learned to hold sadness back by squinting my eyes shut and holding my breath, so I wouldn't upset my mom. I let go and just felt all the sadness I'd been holding back since I was a kid. The odd thing was, once I let go into it, it moved on through and I felt a wave of bliss in my chest. I had an image go through my mind of doves being released to flutter through my chest. It felt great.

"Then something else amazing happened. I realized what had triggered the whole thing was my boyfriend not showing up to bring me something. I realized I was always 'looking for evidence' that people didn't love me, trying to fill some void in me

that was unlovable. I decided to be the source of my own love.
I just stood there and loved myself for ten seconds. I felt really
wonderful, even better than before."

Summarizing

The first Miracle Move is a very simple instruction—use
your consciousness to focus on the natural sensations in your
core zones. Not only is it simple, it's important to *keep it
simple.* If you try to make the move more complicated than
it is, you'll find that it doesn't work.

It's like using a simple box camera: Point at your sensations and click. Easeful or Not?

Easeful? If so, great. You're on the right track.

Not? Point and click again. Hmm . . . it's my stomach
that's tight and fluttery. I must be fearing some sort of threat.
Hmm . . . oh yeah, I'm afraid of getting rejected if I call and
ask Pat out.

One quick "feeling snapshot" will tell you exactly what
you need to know. Then, you can honor the fear of rejection
for a couple of breaths until you begin to flow again. Or just
pick up the phone and make the call. You can't lose. The
worst that can happen is that Pat will actually reject you.
That might awaken some fear in you, or maybe sadness or
longing or anger. But with your Key Move, you're only a few
breaths away from the flow again. It's a miracle, really.

Now that you know how to open up to the Miracle Zone,
are you ready to take that knowledge into the red-hot world
of relationship interaction? It's one thing to practice, but
eventually we need to get out on the field and make the
moves where they count. Where they count most is when

you are with people you care about. Feeling the flow of organic good feeling with yourself is great, but feeling it with loved ones—or even cohorts in the business of daily life—is where the sublime moments of life are to be found.

THE TEN-SECOND MIRACLE IN ACTION

Let's put what we've just learned into action in the real world of relationships. The following example is drawn directly from real life. See if you can relate . . .

The Ten-Second Window

Your partner says, "I'm going to be working late tonight," and you feel a slightly "off" sensation in your body as you hear it. The sensation is a funny feeling in your stomach, but you don't know what to call it. Your old pattern might be to overlook your "funny" feeling. But you've been learning a brand-new way to handle these moments, so you pay attention to your body signals.

Within ten seconds of feeling the sensation, you make a note of it and realize that it's in your fear zone. You're scared about something.

Instead of stewing in it, you say something about your sensations. You report the discovery you've made, and you do it with no blame. You keep it simple:

"I got a funny feeling in my stomach when you said that. I wonder what that's about."

Then you wait for your partner's response. If it is a defensive response, BEWARE. People who respond with defensiveness to statements of truth are unsafe until they can demonstrate an openness to it.

In this situation, the other person got defensive.

YOU: I got a funny feeling . . .

YOUR PARTNER: I don't know why you're so picky. Can't you
    just accept things as they are?

Here are some other ways defensiveness might show up:

Your partner gives you a disgusted look and turns away.

OR

Your partner justifies and explains: "You know we've got
to have that extra money so you can keep going to therapy.
Plus, I was out of the office Monday because Jimmy was sick
and also . . . "

OR

Your partner runs for the victim position: "You know as
well as I do that I hate my job and wouldn't be there unless
we were so far in debt."

Beware of any defensive response. Defensive responses let
you know that something else is going on.

Faced with the defensive response, you realize you're getting action in your anger zone. Your neck and shoulders are
becoming tight.

YOU SAY: Now I'm really getting tense.

YOUR PARTNER SAYS (after a pause): I see what I'm doing. I'm
    getting defensive. Let's start all over. I'm feeling guilty
    about all the time I'm spending at the office. And also,

I'm scared to tell you because I'm afraid you'll just keep getting more critical.

YOU: I see what you mean. I'm frustrated because Jimmy loves his time with you before dinner. When you get here after dinner, he's tired. I hate to see that disappointed look on his face when you're not here for dinner.

Now you're on equal footing. You're out of the defensive mode and communicating as equals, and that's where miracles happen in relationships.

Take a look at a real-life example from a first session with a dynamic woman, age 40, founder of her own advertising agency. Renny has suffered from chronic headaches for many years and has also come in to work on some relationship issues. Her husband has declined to join her for the session. The following interchange takes place after about twenty minutes. I've italicized the places where the Ten-Second Miracle comes into play.

ME: I notice a lot of tension on your forehead.

RENNY: I'm getting a headache right now.

ME: *Let your attention rest on the exact sensations.*

RENNY: A little above my right eyebrow . . . that's where the pain mostly is.

ME: Just feel that area . . . *rest your nonjudgmental attention* on it for ten seconds.

RENNY (does it for ten seconds): . . . Now it's fading.

ME: What do you feel there now?

RENNY: Kind of a flowing, streaming sensation.

ME: Does it feel good?

RENNY: Yes. Definitely better than before. I can still feel sort of the shadow of the headache, though.

ME: Think back over your day. Think if there are any important *One-Breath Communications* you didn't make today. Things you swallowed instead of saying.

RENNY: The first thing that jumped into my mind was something with our biggest client.

ME: Think of the situation and tell me what part of your body tightens up.

RENNY: My shoulders and neck.

ME: That's in the anger zone of the body.

RENNY: Yeah, I guess *I'm angry.*

ME: What would be the simplest One-Breath Communication that would express what you feel?

RENNY: *I'm mad about having to go all the way to Chicago for a two-hour meeting Saturday. I just realized I'm also angry that Ted wouldn't come here with me today.*

ME: *Take ten seconds right now and simply feel the anger without judging it.*

RENNY (after ten-second pause): Okay. That's good. All gone.

One remarkable thing about Renny is her lack of defensiveness. Every time a ten-second window opened up for her, she took full advantage of it. For example, when I invited her to rest her nonjudgmental attention on her headache symptoms, she immediately did it with no resistance at all. I knew right away that Renny's life was going to change rapidly, and it did. She went home from the first session and told her husband that she had made a headache disappear. The next week, he skipped his traditional Monday night football game to join her for a session. She called that a miracle, and, having met her husband, I'm inclined to agree.

THE SECOND MIRACLE:
WHAT TO SAY

*The Ten-Second Communication That
Opens the Flow of Connection in
Relationships*

In the last section you learned how to touch into the Miracle Zone whenever you want. You discovered that you are never more than a breath away from creating breakthroughs in your life. You found that *you can focus your consciousness on your natural feelings and body sensations* to generate a field of miracles from inside you. All these miraculous things are done inside your skin, and that's the place where miracles are born. Now, we need to find out how to extend the Miracle Zone out into our relationships. We need to know how to create miracles in our moment-to-moment interactions with others.

Now, our task becomes . . .

Opening the Miracle Zone in Your Relationships

You'll find that the Key Move you began to practice in the last chapter is crucial to relationships with other people. If we add one other Miracle Move to the Key Move you already have, a circle of miracles forms around you wherever you go.

The Key Relationship Move

Ten seconds is a lot longer than most people think. Not only can you say a lot in ten seconds, you can say anything that *really* needs to be said. In fact, if you take more than ten seconds to say anything important, you're probably doing something extraneous like explaining or justifying. Most important communications in relationships don't need to be explained, and they certainly don't need to be justified. They just need to be said clearly and cleanly. To help you learn to do that, I offer you . . .

The Second Miracle Rule: *Every truly important relationship communication is always said in one breath. Relationship miracles are created when you speak One-Breath Communications that are unarguable and non-blameful.* When you speak a fundamental truth about any issue you face, you create movement toward resolution. You will see positive results within ten seconds.

I've been with many people as they've changed their lives by something they said. Sometimes it was a highly emotional statement, such as "I'm cheating on you." At other times it was calm and resolved, like "I've decided to have the operation." But it was always something that could be said in one breath.

Join me again in my office to feel the power of One-Breath Communications. Notice how simple, almost trivial the italicized communication is. Yet, for this couple, it was the moment that started the healing process:

They duck into my office furtively, their famous faces concealed behind dark glasses and floppy-brimmed hats. The tabloids had covered their romance and their wedding, and now the same media buzzards were circling over rumors of their marital troubles. Owing to the complications of our busy schedules, we had only four hours to get to the bottom of the problem. For the first hour it was heavy going—I felt like a scout picking my way through a minefield of resistance and bristling ego. Finally, in the second hour, we broke through to a moment of truth.

ME: There seems to be something always hovering in the background. Something that needs to be said. I don't know what it is, but I can feel it, like it's haunting us. Do you know what I mean?

SHE: Yeah, I do. It's been there for a long time.

HE: Hmmmph. (His arms are crossed over his chest, and he has a disapproving look on his face.)

ME (to him): I notice your arms are crossed and you have a kind of critical look on your face. What's going on?

HE: Well, um, uh—

ME: What's really going on?

HE: Okay. I'm not committed to this relationship anymore. I'm already gone.

ME: Okay, that's a place to start, but it's not really the unarguable truth. You're here, even though you may be somewhere else in spirit. What's really, really true?

HE (confused, eyes darting back and forth): *I'm scared.*

ME: You're scared. (Out of the corner of my eye, I notice that she has completely dropped her contempt and is looking at him with rapt attention.)

HE (to her): *I'm scared you're going to eat me up. I'm afraid I'll be annihilated.*

That was their Ten-Second Miracle. The moment he said it, they both relaxed visibly. Over the next hour the dialogue took a surprising twist. It turned out they each had exactly the same fear. They both got scared, two months into the relationship, that they were not strong enough to deal with the other's ego. Each had retreated into a fear that they would get overwhelmed. From behind the screen of that unspoken fear, they had thrown rocks at each other for months. They had even enrolled their respective managers in the battle—their managers, who worked for different firms, were embroiled in the conflict on the mundane level of contracts and bank accounts. All because two scared kids—40-year-old kids with hundred-million-dollar bank accounts—were afraid to confront their own inner demons.

Fortunately for them, they turned their relationship around. His ten-second confession was the turning point. Probably to the chagrin of the tabloids, they mended their differences and took their relationship to a new level. I've seen them only at social events since then, but the miracle seems to be holding up well.

Getting Started

So that you can get a feel for the power of simple communications, I'd like you to find out right now just how long ten seconds is. Get a timepiece that can count seconds. While you're watching the seconds tick by, quickly count out loud as high as you can go in ten seconds.

I just paused to do the experiment myself, and got to 34 in ten seconds. Kathlyn looked in the door to see what I was doing, and I asked her to do the experiment. She got to 36.

Now, let's find out how much you can say in one breath. I'm going to take a deep breath and rapidly say the sentence *Mary had a little lamb* on the out-breath as many times as I can. I'm going to count how many times I can repeat it before one out-breath is exhausted. Do it with me, then I'll tell you why it's important.

I said twelve Mary-had-a-little-lambs before I used up one out-breath. Kathlyn said seventeen of them on her out-breath. How did you do?

Regardless of whether you said five or twenty-five, I think you'll agree that you can say a lot with one breath. My colleagues and I have analyzed many sessions, and the Ten-Second Rule applies across the board. Everything important is always said in ten seconds or less. If you speak your communications with certain specific intentions, you'll create miracles even faster. Here's what I mean:

To create relationship breakthroughs, all you have to do is *say anything unarguable that has no blame attached to it. The biggest breakthroughs often come just after communicating something unarguable that's also a fresh discovery. A fresh discovery is something you've discovered within the past ten seconds.* A fresh discovery is something you didn't know ten seconds before.

When you speak brief, unarguable truths, particularly

things you've just discovered about yourself, you will open a field of miracles around you wherever you go.

In the Real World

Let me give you two examples of how to use One-Breath Communications in the real world of interaction. Both of them show the power of these simple, to-the-point communications. The first one happened to me just hours ago.

> ME (to a friend): How are you today?
>
> FRIEND: Fine.
>
> I notice worry lines on his forehead and a bleary look in his eyes.
>
> ME: Gee, I could be wrong, but you don't look fine. You look kind of tired and worried.
>
> FRIEND (startled): Oh. Thanks for noticing—I was on automatic pilot. The baby's got some stomach thing and I was up all night with her.

When I asked the first time, I got a social response. Then, when I mentioned the discrepancy between word and appearance, my friend shifted to an authentic response. His first response—"Fine"—was certainly a One-Breath Communication, but it was arguable. I could see the argument written on his face. Our bodies are very eloquent at telling the truth, and almost everybody sees the truth but politely overlooks it.

The moment my friend made the One-Breath *unarguable*

statement, we entered the zone of intimacy. The walls came down—we were in harmony with each other. Speaking One-Breath Communications is the best way I've discovered for finding out who my friends really are. You can check this out easily in your own life.

If you say to someone "My shoulders are tense" or "I'm scared," watch how he or she responds during the next ten seconds. By speaking a One-Breath unarguable truth, you drop the wall of defense and risk intimacy. You'll find out within ten seconds whether the other person wants to be intimate with you. If the other person says,

Don't be silly—there's nothing to be scared of,
OR
You'll probably feel better in a little while,
OR
Count your blessings that it's not worse,

don't go to that person again for intimacy. At least not until you carefully tell the person what you want in a friend.

If the person says,
Tell me more,
OR
Can I help?
OR
I'm listening,

this person is a safe space for intimacy. You can go there again with your feelings.

THE TEN-SECOND MIRACLE   103

Let me give you a more complicated example that illus-
trates the power of One-Breath Communications, and the
cost of not making them. Come with me into a conference
room high above midtown Manhattan:

I'm sitting with the three top executives of a large corpora-
tion. They've been bogged down in a massive impasse for weeks,
and it is literally costing them millions of dollars a week. I've been
flown in for an afternoon of "emergency surgery." When I enter
the room, all I see are hunched shoulders and angry glares. For
the first hour I try all sorts of strategies to get them moving—
but they mostly snipe at each other and refuse to budge.

Finally, with my frustration growing, I get up and walk over to
the window. I gaze down at scurrying citizens on Fifth Avenue.
I take a few deep breaths and remember to practice what I
preach. It occurs to me that I've gotten so immersed in "fixing"
them that I've forgotten to do the Key Move inside myself. *I let
go of trying to do anything to them and simply tune in to my body
sensations for ten seconds.* I push all thoughts out of my mind and
stand at the window, taking deep, slow breaths and scanning
my body sensations. I discover that my back is tight and stiff, my
throat is clogged, my chest is like an iron fist, and my belly is
tight with fear. Behind me, at the conference table, I can hear
that the quarrelsome conversation has come to a halt. They are
probably wondering, What the hell is he doing?

I turn to face the men and make the Key Relationship
Move—a One-Breath Communication that's unarguable and
not blameful. *I say, "I'm just tuning in to myself. My back is stiff and
my throat feels clogged and my chest is tight and I'm scared. I don't
know what to do."* The three men stare at me, blinking rapidly.
Seconds—and they seem like very slow seconds—tick by.

Finally, one of them says, "I've felt like that for a month." A second one snorts in disgust, and the third one says, "I'm so frustrated I feel like quitting." He stands up and storms toward the door. He stops on a dime and spins around.

"None of you care about this company, do you?" I can see anger on his face, but there's something else, too. It looks like sorrow.

Everybody looks at me again, as if expecting me to say something. They have a right to expect that—they've got ten thousand dollars and a first-class plane ticket invested in this afternoon. But I can't think of anything else to say, so I just take a deep breath and let it go. Another long ten seconds go by as I tune in to my Key Sensation.

"Okay, okay, okay," the top guy says suddenly. "What do we need to do to get through this thing?"

I turn to the man standing near the door. "Frederick, *I notice the anger on your face, but I also see something that looks like sorrow.*"

He stands stock-still for a moment, seemingly stunned.

Finally he says: "*I guess I do feel sorrow.*" He nods. "Yeah, I do. I think of you two like my brothers, and now we'll never get this straightened out."

This odd non sequitur catches my ear. "What happened with your actual brothers?"

"In my family?"

"Yes."

"*Well, they don't speak to each other. They haven't spoken to each other since my parents died.*"

No wonder he can't get through the conflict here in the company. He's got an old family pattern that says you don't get through conflict. As soon as I point this out, he nods his head

in understanding. He's a quick learner, as are many top executives. They don't get up here to the penthouse by being slow to
catch the drift.

He says: "Okay. That was then, this is now."

Twenty minutes later they've not only solved the problem,
they're laughing and shaking their heads about the whole scene.

Notice what happened. First, I tapped into the Miracle
Zone by focusing consciousness on my inner sensations. I
simply felt what I felt, and gave myself a few seconds to
honor my sensations. Then, I said something unarguable,
something I had just discovered within the past ten seconds.
This fresh and unarguable truth triggered another person to
say something unarguable, and the miracles unfolded from
there on out.

It's what I call the "popcorn effect." I've seen it happen hundreds, perhaps thousands of times. But it never fails to impress
me when it works. First, though, one kernel has to pop.
Because of that fact, I have a radical suggestion for you, one that
will help you create a Miracle Zone around you wherever you
go. I suggest that you promote yourself to first kernel in every
relationship you value. *Be the one who starts the popcorn
effect!*

Why? Because the first kernel enjoys the power in relationships! Think of who has more power in relationships: the
person who is willing to reveal the truth or the person who's
trying to hide it? Remember the Watergate affair? Who had
more power in the long run, Richard Nixon or Deep Throat?
The answer is clear: The real power always rests in the hands
of the person who can reveal the truth. It's far better to be the
initiator of the truth than the person who is inspired by the

initiator. Power is a fine thing, but there is a benefit to being the initiator of truth that goes far beyond power. I'm talking about freedom, real freedom. There is tremendous freedom in being willing to speak the truth in key life situations. Why?

Because we human beings define ourselves by how we relate to the truth. If we embrace it, we're free. If we resist it, we can spend our lives running from it. No matter how big a politician or how nimble a running back you are, it's hard to outrun truth. Truth has a way of catching up with you.

This is a secret we should have been taught from the moment we walked into kindergarten: Our lives are shaped by One-Breath Communications we say or don't say. If you dare to take a big breath and say the thing that must be said, you are free. If you hold your breath and swallow the communication, you may never be inspired again in your life. Think of a One-Breath Communication that would have reshaped the course of O. J. Simpson's life. Or Richard Nixon's. Think of the times in your life that a well-timed "yes" or "no" would have changed your direction.

Here's a list of One-Breath Communications that changed people's lives. Notice how elegantly simple they all are:

"I want to marry you."

"I don't love you anymore."

"I don't want to date anyone else but you."

"I want to have a baby."

"I'm not going to be seeing Lynn anymore."

"I've been having a sexual relationship with Sandy."

"I'm angry, and I've been angry a long time."

"I've lost respect for you."

"I've decided I don't want to have children."

"I've made plans to leave immediately if you take another drink."

Communications like these are all unarguably true. When we don't speak the unarguable truth, life shows us nothing but conflict. When we finally get around to saying things that no one can argue with, our lives change rapidly. The argument stops, inside and out.

At a one-week relationship workshop, I invite the group of fifty to spend a few minutes in silence. During the silence I invite them to think of a One-Breath Communication they really need to make.

At the end of the silent period, I ask if they want to tell the group what they've come up with. A man from a foreign country says, in a voice choked with sorrow, that his One-Breath Communication is with his fiancée. He says he has never shared the depth of his heartache over an affair she had. He had tried to be "modern and sophisticated," but it was only an act. He could still feel the aching in his chest, even though it had been a year since the event.

The group took a break, and afterwards he came back to the group looking radiant. He reported that he had phoned her on the other side of the world. He had started a sentence with "I'm so sad," then had paused because he was overcome with sadness. She completed his thought for him. "You're heartbroken over that time I spent the night with Paul." He said yes, and she

said that she had been thinking about the incident just minutes
before his call. He communicated his sorrow to her, and they
both cried. Then she said, "Well, I love you and my heart is open
to you. I'll help you glue yours back together if you still want
me." He said he felt "the weight of the world" gone from his
chest.

....

The deep truths we speak, especially statements like "I'm
having an affair with Sandy," may cause short-term uproar.
But the videotapes reveal something absolutely fascinating,
something I would not have believed twenty years ago: The
upset caused by someone speaking a One-Breath truth seldom lasts even ten minutes. It may come back in waves later,
but it lasts only as long as you resist facing it. The surprising
thing on the videotapes is how often the truth is greeted with
relief. On countless occasions I've seen people say something
like, "Thank you for telling me. I always felt something was
'off,' but I couldn't figure out what."

In thirty years, only one person has actually come back
later and told me she wished she had maintained the lie she
was living with. She had been carrying on an affair for five
years with a friend of her husband's. The guilt was eating her
up and was having ramifications in her family and friendship
network, some of whom knew the truth. In therapy, I counseled her to reveal her secret to her husband, but she quit
after a few sessions without having told her husband. Years
later, I met her at a party, and she told me she had finally confessed. She said she wished she hadn't. She said she missed
the money and social prominence she'd enjoyed, and she
hated having to earn money on her own. I could certainly
understand the practicalities, but on another level I had a

hard time believing her regret. She looked so much healthier than she had when I was seeing her in therapy. Her eyes were lively instead of dull, and her body had a youthful vigor that I didn't remember from a few years before. It's as if our bodies are so relieved by getting out from under the load of the lie that we will put up with considerable short-term inconvenience to be free of it.

Why We Don't Say What Needs to Be Said

Our problems in relationship are largely caused by postponing saying things that need to be said. We usually don't speak these One-Breath truths because we are afraid of taking our listener's breath away. We're afraid of hurting them, which is a polite way of saying we don't want to have to deal with their reaction. If we are to be whole, though, it's a risk we have to take. I've learned, in my own life and as a therapist, that *problems in relationship are caused more by what we haven't said than by what we have said.* Once we take the deep breath and say the One-Breath Communication, our lives will unfold miraculously.

I'll show you what I mean.

My wife, Dr. Kathlyn Hendricks, and I are working with a couple, Lori and Michael.

Michael sits at one end of a couch, his wife, Lori, at the other end. They haven't slept together in six months, and when they finally came in for therapy, it was clear that they were about as stuck as any couple we'd ever seen. Now, in their fourth session, the ice is beginning to thaw a little. The problem is that he has a great deal of unexplored and unexpressed rage. Like most truly angry people, he uses his anger to deny that he's angry and to keep people at bay. She is passive and long-suffering. Although she loves him, she is about to give up.

Kathlyn is encouraging him to let go of denial and accept his anger. This is a man who's been beaten by a drunken father and shot at by Vietcong. He is deeply scarred and wounded—it's as if every muscle of his body is taut with unexpressed rage.

Kathlyn says, "Michael, let go of everything you've been doing for just a moment. Just let go and wonder with me a little. Put your attention on something real that's going on in your body." This catches him by surprise, and he looks up curiously. "Say something true—something you haven't figured out or rehearsed. Just say anything true that's not meant to attack or blame Lori. Say something you've discovered in the last ten seconds."

He looks down at his hands and says, "My palms are sweaty." On the videotape, his wife suddenly looks up—her interest is engaged and she comes out of her defensive posture at the other end of the couch. Next he says, "I don't know why I'm so angry all the time." At this, his wife bursts into sobs. He gives her the first kindly look that's crossed his face. She says, "That's the first time I've ever heard you say anything about yourself like that, Michael."

There is about ten seconds of electric silence. Suddenly he bows his head and begins to cry. It turns out that it's the first time he's cried since watching a buddy die in the Vietnam War.

They went home that day and made love for the first time in months. But that was just the beginning. Within a month he had changed jobs, gotten off psychiatric medication, and turned in an application for graduate studies. Within six months they were talking about having a baby, and a year later Lori gave birth to a baby girl. Michael had once threatened her that if she ever got pregnant he would get an AK-47 and spray Main Street with it. Now he was holding the baby like it was his greatest treasure.

I call that a miracle.

If you watch the tape, you see that everything magical happened as the result of a One-Breath Communication. Michael took wonderful advantage of a ten-second window, when Kathlyn invited him to say something real that he'd just discovered. The explosion of intimacy that followed was, I believe, the positive side of the explosion of rage that he had been carrying. He quietly walked through the minefield of rage into the open arms of his wife, one Ten-Second Miracle at a time.

Let me show you exactly how to create those kinds of miracles.

Every sentence you speak—indeed, every thought you have—serves one of two intentions:

Intention One: *Wondering/Discovering/Learning/Informing/Connecting*

Intention Two: *Attacking/Defending/Making Yourself Right/Making Others Wrong/Justifying Your Position*

INTENTION ONE	INTENTION TWO
Inform	Attack
Discover	Be Right
Learn	Make Wrong
Wonder	Defend
Explore	Justify

In short, every word we say is either about learning or about attacking. Every word we say is spoken in wonder or in fear. Listen to any conversation—on the street, in the office, on television. If you catch any piece of dialogue that's being uttered, you'll find that it's serving one of those two intentions. It will be promoting wonder or putting up walls of defense. It will inform or it will justify. It will be about making a discovery, or it will be about making someone wrong. Learning or attacking—both of them got us to this point in human evolution. From here on out, though, learning is likely to be our best chance of succeeding as a species. I can tell you from personal experience that learning is a much better way to create loving relationships.

When you are feeling stuck or off-center, the quicker you can slip into Intention One, the faster you will restore flow to yourself and the relationship. If you get locked into Intention Two, you do not get to feel the flow of love and harmony. Instead, you get to be right, you get to make others wrong, you get to defend yourself and justify your position.

The administrator of our institute, Gail, gave me a classic example of the choice-point:

"I was spending the evening with my boyfriend, and there came a moment when I needed to tell him something important I had discovered about myself. I could feel myself wanting to tell him, and another part of me not wanting to. I let the moment pass without telling him. Over the next two hours we ended up in a horrible argument. Tracing it back, I can see that everything deteriorated after I chose not to tell him the truth. I spent the next day trying to figure out why I hadn't told him. What I finally figured out was that it was more important to be right and to keep him out than it was to really open up to him."

....

Instead of running from the truth, let's go looking for it.

In my counseling work over the years, I have found that most people would love to be able to tell the truth, if only they knew what it was.

Remember the Key Discovery: *Everything important about relationships is always said in one breath. Big breakthroughs come from communications that are about things you have just discovered, not from communications that blame or justify.*

Any of the Ten-Second Communications shown on the accompanying chart will create relationship breakthroughs! The communication doesn't have to be profound—only authentic. The breakthroughs will occur most rapidly if you communicate within ten seconds of discovering one of the *sensations* listed on the chart.

ZONE ONE

Sensation: Your back (or shoulders, or neck) is getting tense.

Feeling: You're very likely angry or frustrated or aggravated.

What You Need: You need to feel equal. You need to look for what you can do to make that happen.

A Sample Ten-Second Communication: "I'm getting tense and frustrated. What can we do to work together as a team?"

ZONE TWO

Sensation: Your throat or chest is getting tense.

Feeling: You're sad or hurt or longing for something.

Need: You need to face the loss, whatever it is. You need to figure out what you're really longing for.

A Ten-Second Communication: "I'm feeling sad right now. I want to take a moment and feel what I'm losing and what I really want."

ZONE THREE

Sensation: There's a racy, queasy tension in your stomach.

Feeling: You're scared or anxious or nervous.

Need: You need to feel safe. You need to look for what you can do to make that happen.

A Ten-Second Communication: "I'm getting tense and nervous. I want to find out what I'm feeling threatened about. I want to feel safe."

Let's take a closer look at how to use this concentrated package of information.

Zone One

I'm feeling *tension in my back/neck/shoulders . . .*
which means:

I'm *angry (or irritated, aggravated, mad)* . . .
which means:
I've experienced a *trespass.*
And that means:
I need to take actions that allow me *to feel equal.*
If I can do that, I can feel a sense of authentic power flowing through me.

Our research has shown that the best way to feel equal and get others to treat you as equal is to communicate a straightforward statement of sensation or feeling. Communicate from wonder and discovery, not from the position of victim.

What to Say and What Not to Say

■

Example: *Suppose your partner just said he couldn't pick up your son from soccer practice.*

SAY: *I'm just realizing my neck and shoulders feel tight. I started noticing the tension when you said you were not going to pick up Tad from soccer practice.* (Then let silence occur. If your tension releases, stop there. If it remains, speak the feeling of anger. Keep it very simple.)

SAY: *I'm angry.* (Then let silence occur. Don't explain why you're angry.)

The magic is created when you make a simple and unarguable statement of sensation or feeling. If you will give some space and silence after saying it, you'll see powerful results. If you rush in with explanations or excess verbiage, you'll dilute the results.

DON'T SAY: Why don't you ever take any responsibility around here? Why do I have to do everything?

Zone Two

I'm feeling *a lump in the throat/pressure or constriction high in the chest* . . .
which means:
I'm *sad* . . .
which means:
I've experienced a *loss*.
And that means:
I need to *resonate with the reality of my loss*, to say good-bye, even if the loss seems insignificant.
If I can do that, I can open to the organic positive feelings that flow in the chest: love, gratitude, warmheartedness.

■

Example: **Suppose your new lover stops calling. You leave a few messages, using the Ten-Second Miracle Move of communicating your One-Breath feelings to him. Nothing happens. After a few days you are slipping into despair . . .**

DO: Feel for ten seconds the full intensity of your sadness. You may have had great expectations for the relationship, may even have thought that this was the "one." Now the expectation has collapsed and you are in the grip of the loss. The only thing that heals is to face the loss for ten seconds without flinching. You'll know you've done it when the constriction in your throat begins to loosen.

DON'T: Don't distract yourself by raiding the refrigerator or the shopping mall. Don't call your friends and make him wrong. Instead, call your friends and ask them to listen while you express your sadness. When the feeling shifts, thank them and tell them you'll do the same for them the next time they have a loss.

■

I'm feeling *a fist in the chest/uneasy breathing* . . .
which means:
I'm *longing* for something or someone . . .
which means:
I'm experiencing myself as *missing something/incomplete.*
And that means:
I need to take actions toward *union and connection* with myself, another person, or my ultimate fulfillment.

If I can do that, I can meet people heart-to-heart. I can express the passions that are dear to my heart, and I can support others in expressing theirs.

■

Example: Suppose your best friend has just left for a long vacation. You're missing her. You notice the tight-chest sensation of longing.

DO: Focus your attention on the feeling in your chest. Call your friend and tell her (or her answering machine) that you miss her. Open up to what you're longing for. Keep your attention on the longing, and keep looking for the source of it until the fist in your chest releases.

DON'T: Don't distract yourself or talk yourself out of the feeling. Don't compare yourself to your friend, spinning your wheels with envy or competitive thoughts.

Zone Three

I'm feeling *speedy/queasy/uneasy* sensations in my stomach . . .
which means:
I'm *scared* . . .
which means:
I'm experiencing a *threat* of physical or social pain.
And that means:
I need to *take action to remove the threat or create a zone of safety* around me.
If I can do that, I can feel a sense of deep centeredness and ease as I move through the world.

■

Example: **Suppose you are riding in the backseat of a car on a double date. Everyone has had wine with dinner, and suddenly you realize that you personally would feel too tipsy to drive. It's late and raining and there's heavy traffic, so it's not very convenient to get out and walk.**

SAY: I'm scared. I don't feel safe.
DON'T SAY: Are you sober enough to drive?
SAY: Pull over to the curb.
DON'T SAY: Be careful.
If the person won't stop, you'll have to escalate your

demands or at the very least put on your seat belt. In this case, just speaking your fear wouldn't create a zone of safety around you or remove the threat.

Here's a story of exactly how to use the Ten-Second Miracle, both the Key Move that gets you in touch with the truth you're feeling inside, and the One-Breath Communication that delivers the truth to the other person.

Sheila and Les were stuck in a holding pattern about the issue of commitment. Sheila wanted a committed relationship in which they didn't date others. They'd been talking it over for months, and she was getting tired of Les' avoiding the issue. The more she pressed, the more Les said, "I can't be pushed into this."

Finally, one day, the issue strained past the breaking point. Sheila pressed hard and Les backpedaled, all the way to the stage of storming into the bedroom to pack suitcases. Sheila stood in the kitchen, feeling at her wit's end. Suddenly she remembered the Ten-Second Miracle we'd rehearsed in her counseling session. She paused and scanned the three zones of her core sensations. She thought she was angry, but a quick scan of her sensations revealed that she was actually terrified. This came as a revelation to her. She'd been communicating her anger to Les but had not communicated her fear! She also felt some longing in her chest. She took a deep breath and walked into the bedroom, where Les was furiously packing a bag.

"I want to talk," she said. "Can you stop what you're doing and listen?" Les paused and nodded.

"*I'm feeling scared that I'm unworthy—that I'm not worth being committed to. I'm also longing to let go into a deep connection with you.*" Then she returned her consciousness to her body sensa-

tions, to check if there was anything she was overlooking. Les
stared at her for a moment, then took a deep breath.

"Oh," he said, "you're scared. I thought you were just mad at
me."

"No," Sheila said, *"I'm scared there's something wrong with me."*

They looked at each other for a few long moments, then Les
came forward and took her hands. "I want to be with you . . . I
don't want anyone else . . . I'm afraid I'll lose my freedom if I
give myself to you."

As they told me this story, I asked Les to give me more
detail about what had happened in his body and mind when
Sheila told her Ten-Second truth. I knew something major
must have shifted, because his whole stance of avoiding commitment changed in that moment. He told me that it was
like waking up from a trance. Suddenly it was as if he heard
her speaking to him for the first time. He said, "I heard her
real voice, not her critical voice. I realized there was nothing
I needed to fear. Each of us was just as scared as the other.
And I knew we could work it out."

I was inspired by this story, because I believe that people
really are in a sort of trance while they're in relationship conflicts. Usually, the trance has been induced long ago, by how
we saw conflict handled when we were children. The trance
has certain rules of how it has to proceed and how it must
end. And all the rules are totally unconscious. When we do a
Ten-Second Miracle, we break through the trance, and the
breakthrough is almost always contagious.

Once they were out of the trance, Les and Sheila quickly

resolved the issue. The suitcase was unpacked, and when they told me the story the following day, there were tears in their eyes. They made a commitment to each other without struggle or strain, and I attended the blessing of their union on a sunny Saturday in the Bay Area.

As you can see from this example, the Ten-Second Miracle is powerful medicine that heals very quickly. The great thing about it is that it can also be used preventively, as a way of life. After living this way for the better part of two decades, Kathlyn and I have found that we can now spot and prevent most of the problems that used to trip us up.

Before moving on to the next section, let me give you a prescription to keep on your bathroom mirror, dashboard, or refrigerator door:

The Ten-Second Prescription

Find one thing that is absolutely true, and say it in one breath with no blame attached. Keep it simple—make statements like "I'm getting tense" and "I'm nervous" and "I'm hurt" and "I don't know what to say."

If you want to create the most powerful miracles, say the one thing that absolutely must be said to the one person you absolutely must say it to.

I predict that you'll be amazed at the power of this simple move.

THE TEN-SECOND MIRACLE IN ACTION

Resonance, a New Way of Listening to Each Other

If we are going to *speak* One-Breath Communications, we also must be willing to *listen* to them when others speak theirs. In fact, ten seconds of pure listening will produce breakthroughs just as reliably as ten seconds of truthful speaking. My colleagues and I have developed an innovative listening process that adds a great deal of value to standard listening techniques. It's called Resonant Listening, and I want to show you how to use it.

Traditional Listening Techniques

Resonant Listening builds on a skill you may already know and practice: Active Listening. The technique called Active Listening is based on the work of Carl Rogers and was made popular by Thomas Gordon and Haim Ginott in the sixties and seventies. I've taught a variation of it for years, and other variations have been taught by many of today's relationship experts—Harville Hendrix, Allan Ivey, and others. In Active Listening, the listener summarizes and reflects back what he or she has heard to the speaker, giving the speaker a chance to find out if the summary is accurate. The listener not only reflects back the information content of the communication but also reflects back the emotional content.

JOHN: I've been under a lot of stress at work today. I must have gotten fifty phone messages in addition to all the other stuff I had to do. Boy, am I glad to sit down with you and have dinner.

MARY: Sounds like you were incredibly harried today. And
     grateful to have some peace and quiet.

JOHN: You got it.

When it's done well, the speaker doesn't realize it's a technique. Used sincerely, it's simply a way of letting people
know you're with them in mind and heart. When it's done
poorly, it sounds clunky and artificial. I've taught the technique to thousands of people, so I've had plenty of opportunities to see artful and genuine applications of it, as well as
many that set new standards for clunkiness.

The art of Active Listening is in *seeing* the world from the
other person's point of view. The innovation I want to offer
you, Resonant Listening, is based on *feeling* the other person's point of view. You use your whole body as a listening
instrument—not just your ears and mind.

Come into a session with me, as I coach a couple on how
to do Resonant Listening with each other.

MARTY: I think if you criticize me for spending too much money
     again I'm going to scream. I'm just—

JIM: If you had any idea what it costs to run this—

ME: Excuse me. Pause and take a breath or two. It sounds like
     you're both frustrated, and it also sounds like you've been
     down this road before. So let's try something different.
     Would you be willing to do that?

JIM: Yeah.

MARTY: Okay. You're right, this is the same old thing.

ME: Okay. Marty, I want you to speak your mind for ten
    seconds about all this. After ten seconds I'm going to ask
    you, Jim, to give a summary of what she's said. First the
    facts, the words and ideas. Then I'm going to ask you to
    tune in to the feeling under it. Let's give it a try.

MARTY: I'm just so sick and tired of always having to account for
    every penny I spend. I feel like you're always watching me.

ME: That's fine . . . pause right there. Marty, take a few deep
    breaths and rest while you, Jim, summarize the words you
    heard.

JIM: She's saying—

ME: Tell her. "You're saying—"

JIM: You're saying you're sick of me hassling you about spending
    money. Looking over your shoulder . . .

ME: Marty, does that summarize what you said?

MARTY: Yeah, basically.

ME: Okay, Jim, forget about the words for a moment. Tune in to
    the feelings you're hearing. Focus on your body. When you
    hear about her frustration, where does your body
    resonate?

JIM: My shoulders feel tight.

ME: That's your anger zone, so resonate with how angry and
    frustrated she feels. Don't argue with her frustration . . .
    just resonate with it.

JIM (closes eyes and takes a deep breath): Okay . . . I think I can

feel that. It's like a hot, pulling sensation all through my
neck and shoulders. Is that what it feels like to you?

MARTY: Just like that.

JIM: I didn't realize how you felt. I feel like that a lot.

MARTY (lets out a big breath): Oh, honey. Can't we approach
this as friends?

JIM (opens eyes and nods slowly): Yeah, I see what you mean.
We're both frustrated. We're taking it out on each other.

These are the miracle moments that change relationships.
I picked an easy one to use as an example. I can guarantee you
they don't always go that smoothly. Frequently, people dig in
their heels and mount a fierce resistance of some sort. Then,
it's up to the skill of the counselor and the commitment of
the couple to get through the impasse. No matter how long
it takes to get there, though, the actual moment of resonance—the moment that changes everything—only takes
seconds.

THE THIRD MIRACLE: WHERE TO STAND

The Ten-Second Power Shift That Creates Equality and Integrity

For relationships to work, we need to feel equal. We all need to speak to each other as equals and act like we're equal in every possible way. Become equals in your relationships and you become free to create miracles. Unequal arrangements—master/slave, persecutor/victim, controller/pawn—cause everybody to stay miserable for life. This issue is so important that I'd like your permission to go on a brief, passionate rant about it.

Begin by feeling this in your bones: We are all absolute equals. That's the way it is, and that's the way it's always been. It cannot be any other way, for the simple reason that we are all made of the same stuff as everything else in the universe.

You cannot have a relationship with anyone with whom you're not equal. Relationships exist only between equals. If you do not feel equal, you think you're higher or lower, better or worse, more important or less important. And these are all lies of the mind.

An Incredible Temptation

There is a ten-second window when we are all tempted to jump into the victim position in a relationship. It occurs when something we don't like has happened. In those moments, we feel a tremendous pull toward thinking of ourselves as victims. I want you to resist this pull—it can literally kill you. I want you to do something radically different: Quit thinking of yourself as a victim and start thinking of yourself as the full, authentic owner of your life. To do that, you should know about . . .

Three Particular Roles to Avoid

There is a quick way to find out if you are making a relationship problem worse. Ask yourself if you are playing one of three roles: victim, persecutor, or rescuer. Each of these roles is deadly; each makes relationship problems worse. You cannot solve any relationship problem if you are playing one of these roles.

Victim is the most popular role. If you look around you in life, you will notice that most people are eating up their creative energy in dramas of victimhood. They perceive themselves as the victim of something—their boss, the world, their headaches. The energy that's consumed by playing victim is exactly the amount of energy that's required to change their lives.

The moment we put ourselves in the victim position, we have to put something or someone in the persecutor role. This is how we make ourselves unequal, and it causes massive problems. There is no way to resolve a situation when people are thinking of themselves as victims. Ask any personal injury lawyer, "Are your clients ever satisfied, even when they win huge judgments?" I have gone to the trouble of asking this question of quite a few lawyers, and several of them laughed out loud. In fact, they tell me, the exact opposite is true. A large judgment simply cements people more deeply in the perception of themselves as victims. Of course, the other side is doing the same thing at the same time, which is why the legal profession is such a huge growth industry.

I can pinpoint the day my life started changing for the better. It was the moment I stepped out of thinking of myself as a victim and began thinking of myself as fully responsible for my life. Things have never been the same since, and I am very glad.

That's why I want to tell you from the depths of my soul: It is absolutely imperative for you to avoid thinking of yourself as a victim, and equally important to avoid placing other people in the role of your persecutor. But the third role—the rescuer—is also highly toxic to your mental health. When you step into the rescuer role—by being nurse or avenging angel or caretaker—you actually disempower the person you are trying to empower. The rescuer often keeps the whole toxic drama going.

Let's say your best friend calls in a bad mood. "Life is awful and they're doing it to me again." Take care at this moment not to jump into the role of rescuer. To rescue your friend from the bad mood, you might say, "Ain't it the truth? When are you going to get the respect you deserve?" This response might seem compassionate, but it is actually deadly. When you treat other people as victims, you delay their progress toward taking full responsibility for their lives. I don't mean you shouldn't pick up someone who's fallen on the street, donate money to charities, or help people in need. What I mean is that you shouldn't speak to the victim in people and thereby strengthen their sense of weakness. Many of us form our relationships by relating to others as rescuers to their victims, and allowing others to relate to us as victims. I was once coaching a well-known entertainer to stop thinking of herself as a victim (which she did even though she possessed beauty, immense talent, and enough money to give away a million dollars a year for the rest of her life and still have plenty left over). I asked her to weed out any friends from her life that she related to as fellow victims. "There goes my whole Rolodex," she said.

My radical suggestion: Limit your friendships to three or four people who will agree to treat you as fully responsible for your life. Do the same for them. Ask them to tap you on the shoulder, especially when you're upset, and bluntly remind you of the way life works:

- Hey! You're responsible for your life being the way it is. As soon as you realize this, you collect the big payoff: the power to create it the way you want it.

- Hey! There is something you've been overlooking . . . face it right now.

- Hey! Love yourself thoroughly first, and then loving others will be a lot easier.

Let go of the friends who help you blame anybody for anything, because they aren't your real friends. A friend is not someone who helps you think of yourself as powerless—it's a person who reminds you that you are blessed with immense power and it's up to you to use it.

Train your friends to ask you questions like:

What do you need to face and feel?

What's the One-Breath Communication you need to make?

What are you pretending not to know?

What is it you need to learn right now?

What is the crucial choice you need to make?

What action do you need to take?

Let me put this in very personal terms. It's Saturday morning as I'm writing this section. I woke up at 4:00 A.M. to work on it. If I so chose, I could think of myself as a victim for working on the weekend or for not being able to sleep in. But what would be the point? If I occupied the victim position, I would have to view my computer, this book, and the ideas in it as my persecutors. If I so chose, I could go even further with my claim on victimhood: I could envy Kathlyn and Lucy (our cat) for snoozing peacefully in the bedroom while I'm up early with a computer on my lap instead of a wife or a cat.

I could go on a binge of victimhood. I could think of the beautiful garden I'm looking at as a burdensome drain on my resources. I could then go further to think of myself as a hapless champion of order doing battle with the encroaching forces of crabgrass and fountain scum. Once we enter the drama of victimhood, it never ends. That is, it doesn't end until we declare the drama over. And we have the power every moment to declare it over.

You may think that you've heard the last of my rant on victimhood. But I need to ask you to hold on to your hat and fasten your seat belt, because there's one more piece of bad news I must tell you: Do you know what the biggest problem with crying victim is?

It's addictive.

Once you get a taste for it, you have to have a little more every day. It requires time and energy to support the habit, and you have to enroll a band of fellow victims to support you in times of need, which eventually total about twenty-four hours a day.

Now for some good news: Let me tell you how to get out of the victim game. It's a two-step process, and both steps take less than ten seconds.

The Ten-Second Move to Take Control of Your Life

Step One: Declare Yourself in Charge

Make a declaration, first to yourself. For example:

> *I cause my life to be the way it is.*
> *I cause myself to be ten pounds overweight.*
> *I cause all my feelings, whether they are anger or fear or sadness or joy.*

If you don't believe a word of those sentences, that's perfectly normal. Just don't let that stop you from saying them. It absolutely doesn't matter whether you believe them. The metal bars that separate a prisoner from freedom do not care if the prisoner believes he's in jail or not. They clank open and clank closed, and someone else holds the key. The same is true with the me(n)tal bars of victimhood that keep us imprisoned inside ourselves. Break out of jail this minute by declaring yourself free. Say "I'm too stubborn and self-righteous to believe what I'm about to say right now, but nevertheless, I cause my life . . ." Declare "I cause my being in jail," and you'll be surprised how quickly the door swings open.

Step Two: Go Public

It will take you only ten seconds to make the following move: Pick up the phone and ask your closest friend never again to think of you as a victim. Go further, and ask all your friends and family to stop thinking of you as a victim. Tell your friends and family you aren't going to treat them as victims. Ask them when you forget, when you start claiming victimhood, to greet you with, "Wake up! You're in charge. If you don't like it the way it is, make it different. If you don't want to make it different, accept it the way it is." Ask them to hang up on you if you protest. They'll love it, and usually won't have to do it more than once.

Often, this move will thin out your address book considerably. I tell my clients: Surround yourself with three or four people who are absolutely committed to being in charge of their lives. Make an agreement to remind each other when one of you slips into victim thinking. Brainstorm ways of waking each other out of the trance. Victim thinking is habit-forming, and it can

*kill you. It can certainly kill any chances of genuine love
and happiness. On the plus side, claiming full
responsibility for your life is the most exhilarating feeling
I know. It, too, is habit-forming, if you give it a chance to
get established in you. Eventually, if you do it long
enough, you will be surrounded by people who are
coming from a deep sense of personal responsibility and
making a genuine contribution to the world.*

A Secret We All Should Know

I've worked with a few of the wealthiest people in the
world and some of the most famous. A couple of them have
been swollen with self-importance, but most of them were
not. Most of them got the cosmic joke that the whole wealth
and fame thing *is* a joke. Sure they worked hard (in many
cases) to get where they were. Sure they enjoyed (in many
cases) the nice houses and the deferential treatment. But on
another level, they saw absolutely clearly that the wealth and
fame game is entirely a fabrication of the human mind.

Why, then, do we carry on with the fiction of inequality?
It's simple, really. We do it because we feel bad about ourselves. There's only one reason to make up the lie that someone else is better, and that's if we think that we're not so
good. We need to stop doing that, for a very practical reason:
It ruins lives. I've seen inequality ruin a lot of lives. I have
seen a lot of people waste their precious portion of creative
energy in power struggles about who's right, who's wrong,
who gets the bigger office, who gets Mom's attention, on and
on. Fortunately, I've seen equality save a lot of lives, too. I've
seen people recharge their batteries in front of my eyes by

claiming healthy responsibility for something they've been avoiding responsibility for.

If there's one thing I would like you to get from this book, it's the very clear sense that you are absolutely equal with every atom in the universe. Everything is made of the same stuff—whatever you want to call it—and the sooner we feel our deep and equal resonance with the whole of everything, the sooner we can let go of the pretense that there's such a thing as higher or lower, better or worse, more important or less important.

End of rant.

Join with me now as I show you the practical steps of becoming equals with everyone in your life. Join me in taking the hierarchies (and the lower-archies!) out of human existence, so that you can find us all equally holy.

How to Do It

First, wonder. Go around wondering. Many people are looking for wonders, but they forget that *wonder* is also a verb. It can be a lifesaving one. Anything about which we're willing to wonder loses its grip on us. Wondering is one of the best ways of becoming equals with something. Take a dire issue like cancer. If you are ill with cancer, everyone agrees you're the victim of it. It's socially acceptable to think of yourself as suffering from cancer. People will tell you to fight it, that it's you versus It and It is bigger than you. Here's an amazing secret, though—something I wouldn't have believed twenty years ago. I've seen people heal themselves of cancer by taking the radical step of wondering about it. Instead of fighting it, they began wondering about it! They started asking questions like:

What's the real source of my illness?

What can I learn from it?

What's the one thing I need to face that would allow the cancer to disappear?

Sometimes they did not discover answers to these questions for quite a while. You can't beat cancer out of your body with a wonder-question, any more than you can beat it out with criticism, ridicule, or shame. But if you had cancer, wouldn't you rather spend your time wondering than in just about any other state of consciousness?

Wondering is a tool for becoming equals with anything. It's a charming state of consciousness, too—one that you see in the eyes of children, mystics, and wise elders. I'm a cheerleader for wonder. It's gotten me through the toughest times in my life, and I want you to have equal access to it.

Making the Move

There is a Ten-Second Miracle Move that will create lasting equality in your relationships. You bring equality to life by a radical internal shift, which then allows you to greet every moment of relationship—and every person you meet—as an absolute equal.

The Miracle Move is based on the Third Miracle Rule: *You will see miracles happen within ten seconds of shifting to a feeling of complete equality in a relationship. The quickest way to become equal is to claim full, healthy responsibility for any situation that exists, while simultaneously giving others the space to take full responsibility, too. This shift allows everyone to meet on the same level: full responsibility.*

Take a moment right now to feel the following shift in your body.

Whether or not you believe it, say this sentence to yourself: *I am equals with everything and every person in the world.*

Say it a few times until you feel this fact "click in" down in the cells of your body. Once you feel that you are made of the same stuff as royalty and the trees and the person next door, you are ready to make another radical shift. This one will eliminate most of the pain from your life if you fully make it.

Here it is:

The only way to feel equal with other people is to acknowledge yourself as fully and completely responsible for everything that happens in your life—*and then to acknowledge other people as fully and completely responsible for everything that happens in theirs.* The only level meeting ground between us is when I am claiming 100 percent responsibility and you are claiming 100 percent responsibility. If I edge over the line even to 102 percent, I skid in the sticky direction of martyrdom or bullyhood. If I make a tiny slip to 98 percent, I sink my foot into the quagmire of victimhood. But oh, the magic of landing right on the line—the miracle of coming into clean, clear 100 percent responsibility! Watch what happens within seconds when you acknowledge complete responsibility for something. The moment you say to yourself, "I accept full responsibility for [any situation]," feel the sensation of exhilaration and relaxation flow through your body.

Notice the reactions of people around you. Watch the look

on your lover's face when you say, "You know that problem we've been discussing? I've decided to take full responsibility for it." Notice the looks on your colleagues' faces when you step up and say "I take full responsibility" for anything that emerges at work. You will see a new spirit break into being around anyone who claims healthy responsibility.

Our big fear is that we will take responsibility and the other person won't. But having helped hundreds of people move through this fear, I can give you some good news: People get inspired by someone who takes healthy responsibility.

I've been witness to miracle moments like the one in which a woman took a deep breath and said to her husband: "You know how I've been blaming you for having that affair? Well, you're certainly responsible for going to that hotel with her, but my part is that I got so immersed in the kids and their activities that I stopped thinking of me or you as a sexual being. I created this crisis by just not paying attention. It was inevitable."

That kind of awareness takes a rare form of courage. It's a type of courage that usually doesn't make the front page of the newspaper. Yet it is truly the stuff that heroic lives are built on. In this example, the couple stopped fighting about the affair and focused their attention on finding out what their mutual goals were. They reinvented their marriage before my eyes. I'm not saying it was easy or that it happened overnight, but the key movement began—and always must begin—with the courage to make the Ten-Second Miracle Move in the conversation I quoted.

In my office a couple may be arguing about money. Suddenly one of them breaks out of the conflict trance and says,

"I will take full responsibility for planning for our financial abundance." The other one may react with surprise or confusion or disbelief, but almost never does the person say, "Great, then I can stay on the couch all day." What saps energy is the power struggle over who's responsible. Once someone—anyone!—claims responsibility, the whole energy field around the problem begins to shift in a positive direction.

The best place to feel the effects of healthy responsibility, though, is with the positive shift in your internal sensations. If you are paying attention, you'll feel a streaming sense of well-being after you claim healthy responsibility for anything. You truly have to feel it to believe it.

Let me give you two brief examples of how to take personal responsibility. Then I'll tell you a personal story, a Ten-Second, one-hundred-pound Miracle moment that changed my life.

> Imagine that you are watching a movie in a theater and the focus on the screen goes slightly off. You sit there in uncomfortable silence for a moment, then the mutters begin. Eventually someone stands up and takes responsibility for getting it fixed. Instead of stewing in silent complaint, someone stands up and takes action. Wait a moment! Isn't the projectionist responsible for adjusting the focus on the movie screen? Apparently not, based on the results you can see on the blurry screen. Adjusting the focus may be in the projectionist's job description, but he's certainly not responsible until the moment he takes responsibility. In the meantime, you can fester for an hour in complaint, or you can get up and take

responsibility yourself. Pick one. For me, I'd much rather make the trek into the lobby than sit there watching an out-of-focus movie.

Imagine that you are in an argument with your lover about whose fault it is that the electricity has been shut off. You say it's her fault that the bill didn't get paid; she says it's yours. Suddenly you both wake up and realize that this argument could go on for days. You make a Ten-Second shift and both of you claim responsibility for the problem. You look at your contribution, and she looks at hers. End of power struggle. You decide to put your energy into getting the lights on instead of figuring out who's right.

In 1969 I was more than one hundred pounds overweight. Obesity ran in my family, and I followed in the family tradition. First I was a fat kid, then I became a fat grown-up. I had a story about why I was fat: I was genetically doomed by fat parents and grandparents, I had thyroid problems, and so forth. I could tell this story to anyone at the drop of a hat. Not many people were interested, but I always had my story ready anyway. Then one day I woke up. I realized that having a good story about why I was fat was not helping me lose weight. In fact, I saw that my story might kill me. Obesity had contributed to my father's early death, and I seemed to be replaying his tragic life-script. So I made a Ten-Second decision that changed my life.

I stood alone on a snow-swept New England country road and took a silent vow. I committed to creating and enjoying a healthy body, regardless of what other people in my family had done with their bodies. I vowed to break free of my script by writing a new one of my own. In my new script, I took personal charge of my well-being and released all others, living or dead, from any responsibility for my health. I vowed to do whatever it took to create a healthy body.

Within a year I had lost close to a hundred pounds, with more pounds coming off later. Because I accomplished this task, I know in my bones that it's possible to change a life-script (and a heavy one, indeed) by a Ten-Second move. This is the move that we all need to make to create any change in our lives. All that is ever required is that we take full responsibility for creating the change—not as a burden and not because we think we're obligated, but because we just do, for no reason other than the doing of it.

The Ten-Second Prescription

There is really only one secret to becoming equals, now and forever: Notice anything you're complaining about— silently or out loud—and claim full responsibility for its existence in your life. Take a deep breath and say, "I cause this to be happening." Go further and end the victim drama for all time by saying, "No matter how much I might protest, I am always responsible for the way my life goes."

The moment you take this radical step, you're free. Not only are you free, you've stepped into the power spot in the universe. When you and I claim responsibility for creating and maintaining any problem we have, we get to enjoy the payoff: the power to change the problem, to create life anew the way we want it. Knowing that changed my world. Knowing it will change yours.

If enough of us know it, nothing can stop us from creating a better world.

TEN-SECOND BREAKTHROUGHS FOR THE SEVEN BIGGEST RELATIONSHIP MISTAKES

PART TWO

SPOTTING THE TEN-SECOND WINDOWS WHEN MIRACLES ARE EASIEST TO CREATE

In part 2 we will take the Ten-Second Miracle into the real world of relationship problems. In daily life, only a small number of relationship situations account for most of the problems. These are the moments that cause the most misery if not handled correctly. I want to show you the techniques I know to works miracles in these situations. In some cases I'll even give you dialogue suggestions, based on what I've seen works best. In the beginning, you will probably want to follow the dialogue suggestions closely. Later, you will probably want to innovate, to improvise your own moves based on the general principles that are at work. Think of the process as you would a new athletic skill: Practice the fundamentals until you can do them in your sleep.

An Amazing Lack

It's still amazing to me that we receive so little training in how to handle the most crucial moments of our relationship lives. Think of the moments that matter most in life—when you first meet someone, when you're stuck in a conflict and can't get out, when you're feeling distant, when you're trying to solve a problem without blaming the other person. Isn't it remarkable that we didn't practice dealing with those situations when we were in school? Once, sitting near the tennis courts at a hotel, I watched a professional tennis player practice his drills. The coach would hit him a very high shot and the pro would smash it down the line. This went on for an hour! Later, in conversation, he said that he tried to hit one hundred or so of these shots at each practice session, along with all his other key shots. I wish I could have spent even one hour in school with a coach lobbing difficult relationship situations at me. I could have saved myself and others a lot of pain if I'd known how to communicate my feelings, listen to others, shift out of blame, and handle my anger better.

What Is a Ten-Second Window?

Learning to recognize ten-second windows can be one of the most important things you'll ever do. I recommend putting it at the very top of your priority list of lifelong learning goals. The reason is this: Right after something has happened is the best time to deal with it. If you break a glass in the kitchen, *right now* is the perfect time to sweep up the pieces. If you don't, two things happen.

First, you've got it on your mind that you left something undone. Part of your mind becomes occupied with it, and you can't put your full attention on your current task. Second, if you leave the broken glass on the floor, someone can come along and get hurt. The same thing holds true throughout your life: When you start to drift off course, a quick correction can save a lot of trouble down the line. The automatic pilot of an airplane is a good metaphor to think about when learning about ten-second windows. The moment a plane begins to swerve off course, the autopilot registers the drift and corrects it. Then if a drift occurs in the other direction, the autopilot catches it and corrects again. The plane is probably exactly on target less than 10 percent of the time. Most of the time it's drifting off course and catching the drift. In other words, a plane can take off from San Francisco, be wrong 90 percent of the time for the next few hours, and still land safely in Honolulu.

The autopilot is a great gadget to have on board—not because it's perfectly on target all the time, but because it's quick to catch the drift. In this imperfect world of ours, we're always going to be drifting. The only thing that counts is whether we catch the drift! That's very good news for you and me. We don't have to be right all the time to hit our targets in life and work and love—we just need to be quick to catch the drift. And the ten-second window is where and when the drift begins to occur.

As an example, let's use a moment that occurs millions of times a day.

A friend greets you and asks, "How are you?" In actual fact, you are feeling tired and headachy. In the ten seconds following the question, either you speak the truth of how you actually feel or you settle for a socially acceptable "Fine."

Your ten-second window is after the "How are you?" What you say here determines whether or not the relationship will

become more intimate. I'm not saying you should be intimate with everyone who asks "How are you?" What I am
saying is that these ten seconds determine whether you will
be more intimate with the person.

If you say "I'm tired and headachy," you move toward intimacy. *This immediately opens another ten-second window.*
Now, your friend determines whether he or she wants more
intimacy with you. The spontaneous reaction will tell you all
you need to know. If the person responds with "Tell me
more" or a facial expression that's open and interested, you
know you are in a welcome space for intimacy. If the person
says "Get over it" or "Take an aspirin," you should probably
look elsewhere for intimacy.

This ten-second window is also the time in which unfinished business is created. If you say "Fine," you have set a lie
in motion. You are feeling one thing and saying another. You
can get away with this sometimes—but only in the sense that
you don't always get caught. You can never get away with a
lie in another sense—the actual reality of how you feel in
your body. If you say "Fine" and are really feeling tired and
headachy, your body registers the lie and stores the information. The person you lie to goes into the large file in your
mind called People I Lie To, which is synonymous with
another large file called People I Am Not Intimate With.

Even if you sleep next to a person every night for twenty
years, you still may not be completely intimate with that person, because there are withheld truths that divide the bed in
half. I have worked with long-married couples who have discovered, sometimes to their horror, that they have never experienced the genuine intimacy that comes from being completely honest with each other. Once when I was discussing

this issue on a talk show, the host blurted out in wonderment, "I don't think I've been intimate with anybody in my whole life!" When the show aired, however, I noticed that this moment of intimacy had been snipped out.

The ironic truth is that the other person's body usually registers the lie, too—just as our own bodies register it when other people lie to us. We may not register the lie consciously, but some part of us usually knows when there's something "off" in the communication.

The unfinished business that is often set in motion by seemingly trivial social lies sometimes has time- and energy-consuming consequences. Continuing with the earlier example . . .

> You say "Fine" and your friend says, "Glad to hear it. See you later." You go your separate ways. A few minutes later you are in your office, but you find you can't concentrate on your work. You realize it's nagging at you that you didn't tell your friend exactly how you were feeling. At the same moment your friend is in another office, wondering what didn't feel right about the interchange. Your friend registered a disconnect between your "Fine" and a pinched look on your forehead. Suddenly your friend realizes that you said "Fine" but were wearing a different look on your face. The two pieces of information don't match.

At this point there is another ten-second window—when you realize there is unfinished business. One Ten-Second Miracle Move right now would be to pick up the phone and say, "I told you this morning I was fine, but I'm really tired and headachy. It was bugging me that I wasn't authentic with you." Your friend would reply, "Whew, thanks for telling me. It felt like something was wrong." Or your friend might pick up the phone and say, "I noticed a pained look on your face this morning. You said you were fine, but I'm wondering if you're hurting."

If this ten-second window is overlooked, further unfinished business can be created.

> As you think it over, you decide that your friend is not as much of a friend as you thought. You decide that he or she is not really trustworthy and that it was right to fake it. Meanwhile, in the other office, your friend is having similar thoughts. Interpretations rush into your minds about each other, most of them negative in tone. You both take a step back from each other in your hearts and minds.

The further you go from the ten-second windows and the Miracle Moves that can enrich them, the more likely you are to experience distance and interpretation. *We usually do not see that it's our own failure to make a Miracle Move that creates the distance and the negative interpretations.* We usually think it's something about the other person. It never is.

I'm not saying that other people can't be petty tyrants, scofflaws, rapscallions, thugs, and cutpurses. Many of our fellow citizens can be royal pains, from their dandruff down to their bunions. What I'm saying is that when we overlook the ten-second windows, we carry the overlooked material home with us, stored in cramped muscles and worry-thoughts.

Watch for the windows, make your Miracle Move, and you can go home without excess baggage.

Catch You Later

What happens if you notice a ten-second window when it's not convenient or socially appropriate to say anything about it? This happens a lot in life. You notice your boss berating a fellow employee, you feel deeply uncomfortable, and yet you don't want to say anything because you're bucking for a promotion. When this sort of thing occurs, for whatever reason, there are two moves to make. One is required, the other is optional.

The required move is to handle it in your own body.

- Notice the sensations or feelings and name them silently to yourself.

  My back is tight . . . I'm angry.

  I feel racy-queasy . . . I'm scared.

  I feel a lump in my throat . . . I'm sad.

  I feel tight in the chest . . . I'm longing for something.

- Breathe some life into the sensations you feel. Three good breaths will usually do it. This keeps you from carrying the feelings home with you.

The optional move is to make a note to communicate about it later. This might mean . . .

—Expressing your sadness, fear, and anger to your boss. This courageous move can often produce huge breakthroughs (and it can sometimes produce massive backfires).

—Expressing your sadness, fear, and anger to your colleague. This move requires skill of a different kind. You must avoid treating the person like a victim. The moment you lock into a victim/persecutor interpretation of any event, you become a coconspirator in a drama that never ends.

There is a way out, though, and fortunately for all of us, it never takes longer than ten seconds.

THE FIRST MISTAKE

You feel "off" inside and take it out on people around you.

Your first relationship concern *is your relationship with yourself.* If you don't feel a flow of organic good feeling inside, you're likely to take it out on everybody around you. When we slip into bad moods, we suddenly start seeing the world as a dark and evil place. People seem twisted, full of dire motivations. Later, when our mood improves, the world looks brighter. We look around at our fellow citizens and think, What a fabulous bunch we are!

Once upon a time I was visiting a friend who is a classic-car buff. I noticed an old car parked in his driveway. Not knowing much about cars, I asked if it was a classic of some kind. It just looked like an old car to me.

"Well," he said, "when I'm in a good mood I think it's a classic. When I'm not, it's a wreck."

It's the same with our relationships! When we're in a great mood, we look at our partners and think we're the luckiest people alive. When we're in a bleak mood, we look at the same fabulous partner and think "fixer-upper." When we're in a bad mood, we don't see who the real fixer-upper is.

Our first concern, then, is with keeping the flow of good feeling going in ourselves. And here, the Ten-Second Miracle can work wonders.

Misguided people reach for an artificial solution to restore the flow of good feeling. In my misguided days I would stuff a fistful of cookies in my mouth or try to make someone else the cause of my bad feeling. Truly stupid people reach for an artificial solution that has addictive properties. In my truly stupid days I smoked an average of two cigarettes an hour during my waking hours. Maybe the first few times I "smoked for pleasure," as the advertisement says, but after that I smoked to keep a bad feeling at bay. What a chump I was. Only a chump would come up with the solution of making himself sick all the time to avoid feeling bad.

The best way to get the flow of organic good feeling going again is to do a Ten-Second Miracle Move in one of your three core zones. Keep it simple and it will always work.

How to Do It

Let's say you get out of bed some morning not feeling the flow of organic good feeling. You want to feel good. You have important things to do, and you'd like to bring fresh, flowing energy to your activities. What should you do?

Scan your three core zones. When you do, you discover that you feel tension in two of them. As you tune in, you realize you feel tension in your throat and your shoulders—that's the exact sensation that lets you know you're feeling "off." Before you did the scan, you just knew you weren't feeling good. Now you know something much more specific: What you're really feeling is "no flow" in your shoulders and throat.

The Ten-Second solution is to rest your consciousness on the zone that feels most blocked, and to let it rest there for a few seconds until the blocked sensation starts to shift. It will start to shift toward flow after a few seconds—it has to. The reason: The consciousness you are focusing voluntarily will reach toward the consciousness around and behind the blocked sensation.

The flowing sensation is already there. It was happening all the time. You just couldn't feel it because it was overshadowed by the tension. As soon as you go looking for it, though, it will reward you richly.

Consciousness is already in existence everywhere—it's your organic gift. *And*, your ability to place your consciousness voluntarily is a talent that can be practiced and cultivated. When you voluntarily place your consciousness on a particular place and let it rest there, it begins to call forth the consciousness that's already permeating the place. Space and consciousness are always there, even in the middle of the tight spots, but we can't feel the space and consciousness because they are overwhelmed by the tension or pain in the area.

The important thing to remember is this: *The moment you rest your nonjudgmental attention on the tension or pain for ten seconds, you create an opening for miraculous transformation.*

To see how much power this move generates, marvel at the story of Ken Hecht, a television producer who shared the following experience in *Newsweek*. I was so moved by his story that I wrote him a "fan" letter and began a correspondence with him. Ken had struggled with obesity for a long time, until he broke the cycle in a Ten-Second Miracle moment.

"For me the key to breaking the cycle [of binge eating] was to finally decide one night to give in to the anxiety. Not numb it with the food, but instead go, rather than eat, cold turkey. I wanted to just sit there and see if the nightmarish anxiety I so feared would in fact total me. So I sat and felt god-awful and eventually felt feelings of self-loathing and disgust and worthlessness. And finally the panicky desire to eat passed. It lasted less than 30 minutes. It was an awful experience, and one that I highly recommend. Sit with yourself. Don't eat, don't go to a movie, don't turn on the television. Do nothing but sit quietly, be miserable and feel what you're terrified of. . . . It is part of yourself you need to know.

"Doing this just once changed my life."

Ken proceeded to lose more than 120 pounds. He didn't lose the weight overnight and he didn't eradicate the pull toward binge eating, but as he put it, there were "many times when the anxiety came and I drew on that one experience and knew I could tough it out."

The Ten-Second Miracle occurred when he turned to face and feel the anxiety. Facing it for ten seconds gave him the strength to do it for another ten seconds, and the strength kept increasing as he stood in the face of his lifelong pain for a half-hour! When you have 120 pounds to lose, it's going to take a succession of Ten-Second Miracles for months or even years. The good news is: All you have to do is start with one Ten-Second Miracle, and that will give you the power to create another one. Your life will unfold in waves of miracles, ten seconds at a time.

The Ten-Second Prescription

When you feel off-center, scan the feeling zones of your body: Zone One—upper back and neck; Zone Two— throat and chest; Zone Three—belly. Feel where the constriction is most unpleasant. Where do you feel most stuck? Find the stuck place and feel the sensations for ten uninterrupted seconds. Just feel. Within ten seconds you will begin to experience a flowing sensation where the stuckness was. If your awareness slips off, keep coming back until you feel the flow begin around and behind the stuckness. If you keep your awareness on the flowing sensation, you will feel it blossom into spacious openness. This is the Miracle Zone.

THE SECOND MISTAKE

*You don't know how to connect
authentically with people when you
first meet, so you start off relationships
on the wrong foot.*

The Ten-Second Miracle is perfect in first meetings. By meeting in the Miracle Zone, you open up a clear field of unlimited possibility from which you can create something brand-new. If we don't meet people from the M-Zone, we are highly likely to imprint our first meetings with the habits and patterns of the past. Your Approval Seeker might shake hands with his Controller. Her Suffering Martyr might fall into the arms of your Caretaker. Until you're completely enlightened, whatever that is, some of this Persona-to-Persona meeting is probably unavoidable. So be gentle with yourself if you fall into Persona-traps in first meetings. Set the goal, though, of learning to meet people free of the old patterns acquired earlier in life. If you commit yourself body and soul to meeting people in the M-Zone, in what I call the *radiant reality of the present moment,* you are more likely to create magical relationships in which you get what you need and so do they.

How to Do It

In the first ten seconds of meeting another person, *say only things that are unarguably true, and say things that you've just discovered in the past ten seconds.* By meeting people that way, you'll know you're in the radiant reality of the present moment. You'll be telling the full authentic truth, and you'll be communicating fresh discovery. Your relationship will start in a clear space of authenticity and zest.

What does this look and sound like in the real world? Let's play a conversation as it might ordinarily go, then replay it using a Ten-Second Miracle.

> You're standing at the punch bowl at a party. An interesting-looking man comes up beside you. You glance at him and he smiles.
>
> HIM: Hello.
>
> YOU: Hi.
>
> HIM: Great party, huh?
>
> YOU: Oh yes. Jim and Diane are such a lovely couple.
>
> HIM: Good punch?
>
> YOU: Sure looks good. Want some?
>
> HIM: Sure.

I hope none of my readers nodded off while reading this bit of dead-boring dialogue. Yet that's often the kind of conversation that people use to begin their relationships. Now, let's bring life to the party with a Ten-Second Miracle opening. We'll keep "Hello" and "Hi" intact, but notice that every bit of dialogue that follows is true and comes from a discovery made within the past ten seconds.

HIM: Hello.

YOU: Hi.

HIM: I notice you're studying the punch.

YOU: I'm trying to figure out if I want any or not.

HIM: When I do that, I realize I'm not even thirsty.

YOU: Me neither.

HIM: I'd like to sit down and talk to you though.

YOU: Me too.

Notice that in the first conversation you met each other as social personas talking mask to mask. There was no discovery and no authenticity in the conversation. When people come in for therapy—after they have hit the wall in their relationship—they inevitably complain about a lack of authenticity and discovery in the relationship. But looking back to the moment they met, they will often realize that none was there from the beginning.

Let's do it another way. Get in the habit of saying only things that are true and fresh when you meet someone new. Saying fresh, true things will have two results, both incredibly useful. First, it will ground the relationship in authenticity and discovery from the very beginning, giving you something real and exciting to build on. Second, and equally important, it will flush out people who do not have good potential for authenticity and discovery. They will react poorly to both of these kinds of statements. If they are allergic to the excitement of truth and discovery-in-the-moment, they will get rattled or backpedal away from you. It's a great time-saver for you. If you are committed to authenticity and self-discovery, you won't want to spend much time around people who aren't interested. Every moment you spend around a fixer-upper project is a moment you're not available for what you really need.

Keep your first meetings simple. If everything you say is true and freshly discovered, you cannot go wrong. Don't overload these precious initial moments of contact with the excess baggage of false fronts or small talk. You'll go home not knowing yourself any better and not having truly met anyone soul-to-soul. You'll end the evening feeling all talked out and very, very small. Instead, surf the edge of genuine aliveness, the kind that can come only from being right there in this moment with your authentic self.

The Ten-Second Prescription

When you first meet someone, stay in the present. Don't run agendas and patterns you've used before. Say only things that are unarguably true, even simple things like "I'm feeling warm in here" and "I feel nervous about being here." If you make fresh statements—things you've just discovered within the past ten seconds—you'll charge the conversation with spontaneity and see miracles unfold before your eyes.

Try what I'm suggesting today or tomorrow. You won't believe the power of something so simple.

THE THIRD MISTAKE

*You feel tension and distance in
a relationship and don't know how
to get unstuck.*

I imagine you've endured moments such as the one I'm about to describe. I have.

> You're with a spouse or lover in the evening, and as the hours wear on you're still stuck in exactly the same "vapor lock" of distance and tension that was there when you got up this morning. There's a coolness, a wariness—something's off but you can't put your finger on exactly what. The minutes tick on . . . the tension remains . . . you want to do something to relieve it but you can't figure out what to do.

I hate these times. A kind of desperate feeling sets in, like hearing fingernails on a chalkboard. I start wondering if I'm going to shatter inside, like a china cabinet in an earthquake. For thirty years I've been opening my office door and seeing that desperate look on couples' faces. I know what they've been feeling, and my heart goes out to them. Let's find a better way.

How to Do It

Good feeling stops flowing when we lock into our stubborn positions. "You're wrong." "I'm right." "I'm a bigger victim than you are." Once we're stuck in a position, we have no freedom of movement. Plus, the other person usually takes an equally rigid position. When movement ceases, we are in the same fix as a body without blood circulation. All systems go downhill fast.

When you're feeling stuck, the first thing you have to do is get the circulation going. The best way to do that is to focus on the main feeling zones of your body: belly, chest, upper back/neck/shoulders. Remember, these zones are where we feel fear, sadness, and anger. When we are out of touch with the flow of energy from these zones, we get stuck quickly. In other words, when we're angry and don't know it, we get stuck. When we don't know we're sad or scared or longing for something, we are entering logjam territory. Once you're stuck, there's a tendency to do more of what got you stuck in the first place rather than shifting to a new strategy. You've probably noticed that. When mired in an argument about who's right and who's wrong, for example, many people escalate their contention that the other person is wrong. Of course, this never creates a breakthrough—only a deeper logjam.

There is only one reliable way out of a logjam: the Ten-Second solution. Keep it simple and keep it short: *When you make a One-Breath feeling statement from any of these zones, the tension begins to dissolve. The farther down the body you go (from top to bottom), the quicker the tension releases.* In other words, a statement about fear will break up the logjam quicker than a statement about anger. However, you must start by speaking the feeling from whichever zone feels most sensation in it. Don't try to fish for a feeling along the front of your body if you're focused on the feeling of anger in your upper back and shoulders. Say the one that's strongest first; then that one will release and you'll have access to others.

Remember this key piece of information: *The tension will release most quickly when the feeling statement is something you've discovered within the past ten seconds.*

Listen to a dialogue between two people who are not speaking One-Breath statements from their feeling zones, nor are they speaking things they've just discovered. Then, watch what happens when I ask them to shift to the Ten-Second Miracle techniques.

BOB: Whenever you do that, when you talk to Amy (their daughter) in that tone of voice, I just want to wallop you one. I never would, but—

RACHEL: See! There's always that threat in the background—

BOB: I would never—

RACHEL: Maybe not, but—

ME: Whoa! Pause right there, please . . .

They pause and glare at each other, then at me.

ME: Pause and take a few breaths . . . shift your attention into your own bodies . . . you could go on like that all day—

RACHEL: He's been going on like that for months—

BOB: Me! You're the—

ME: Halt! Just take a break. You know no one's going to win that one, so let's do something new. Pause and keep your attention focused inside your skin for long enough to take three deep breaths.

They follow my instructions. By the third breath, their expressions have softened. This is the first Ten-Second Miracle working. They have shifted their attention to something real—what's going on in their bodies.

ME: You both sound angry. What are you feeling up in your neck and shoulders?

BOB: Just kind of tight.

RACHEL: Yeah. Tight.

ME: That's in the anger zone. Say "I'm angry" a few times to each other, until you feel your shoulders start to relax.

BOB: I'm angry.

RACHEL: I *am* angry.

BOB: I'm *angry*.

RACHEL: I'm angry.

They both take spontaneous deep breaths and settle more into themselves.

ME: Check into these other places in yourselves (I point on a chart to the feeling zones of sadness, longing, and fear) and feel what's going on there.

Now the magic begins to happen. Rachel will shift the energy
of the whole session with a One-Breath Communication.

RACHEL: I'm longing for that connection we had before Amy
was born.

BOB (looking bewildered): But everything's different now.

RACHEL: I know that intellectually . . . I just miss what we had
. . . spending a whole evening snuggling.

BOB (nodding, suddenly realizing what Rachel is saying; at this
moment they shift from being enemies to becoming allies):
Now we don't get a hug without getting interrupted.

They take another spontaneous deep breath and move a
half-step toward each other. They start to smile.

I find moments like these deeply moving. Although I've
beheld them almost every day for the past few decades, they
always seem brand-new. I think it's because there is an ele-
ment of rebirth in these moments—springtime is appearing
in the hearts of people who've been frozen in winter sleep,
sometimes for years.

The Ten-Second Prescription

*When you're stuck in a relationship impasse, there's
only one way to freedom. You must feel what's true inside
you and speak the truth at the deepest level you can
muster. The simpler you can say it the better—truth
needs no explanations or justifications. Say only things
that can be delivered with one breath, and say things that*

come from your body's main feeling zones. Simple, brief communications— "I'm hurt" and "I'm so scared" and "I'm feeling achy in my chest"—are the stuff of which breakthroughs are made. They need no embellishment. The power of authentic truth, simply delivered, gives you everything you really need.

THE FOURTH MISTAKE

You don't know whether to leave or stay in a relationship, and you stew in indecision while other things in your life fall apart.

How do you know when it's time to leave? Kathlyn and I have encountered this question so often in so many cultures—from Boston to Berlin to Bombay—that we simply refer to it as The Question. Here's the dilemma: If I leave, am I leaving in the grip of some pattern that I'll just repeat later with someone else? How do I make sure I've done everything I can to heal *this* relationship before I go through the pain and destruction of breaking up?

There is a simple Ten-Second way to answer this question. You have to be courageous enough to ask two questions, and you have to be willing to let your *body* answer. Our minds are very unreliable in situations like this. These are the same minds that will persuade us to run back into a burning building to get our favorite shoes, the same minds that inspire us to take our paychecks down to the gambling casino. To find out whether you should take your body out of a relationship, you must let your body do the talking.

I once asked an abused woman, "Why did you move back in with the same husband who beat you up four times already this month?" I was exasperated by her choice and also feared for her life.

She said: "My body was screaming 'Don't go back,' but I thought maybe he was improving, maybe I ought to give it another chance. It just seemed like the right thing to do."

In difficult dilemmas like this, our bodies are not only our Oldest Friend, they are sometimes our only friend. Often our social network polarizes into two camps—those rooting for us to stay and those rooting for us to leave. I've been there myself, and I felt as if I were in the center of a tug-of-war. After ending a difficult relationship in my mid-twenties, I had one set of friends that said "What took you so long?" and another group that said "You're making a big mistake!"

Sometimes our friends are motivated by compassion for us, but sometimes they are also motivated by fear. When one couple breaks up, it sends ripples through their friendship network, causing everyone else to ask hard questions about their own relationships.

The First Question

The first question I ask people to consider—not in their minds but in the depths of their bodies—is:

Has the pain in the relationship overshadowed the possibility of it, or has the pain snuffed out the possibility completely?

Let me take you inside a lecture hall, where the following interchange was captured on tape. A sorrowful-looking woman about 40 years old stood up and asked The Question. There was an electrifying silence in the room.

I think everyone knew she was asking it sincerely and for her own survival. It was clear from her slumped shoulders and wide eyes that she was in despair and confusion about which way to turn. Notice how she finally answered her own question.

> WOMAN: Part of me's screaming "Get Out Get Out Get Out," but another part of me wants to make sure it's the right thing. Do you know what I mean?

> ME: I surely do. I've been there myself. Also I've seen a lot of people come up against that.

> WOMAN: So how do I find out?

> ME: Start with where you are right now. Scan your whole body and feel everything that's going on inside. Be very gentle and nonjudgmental with yourself—like taking a sounding inside your body.

> WOMAN: Okay.

> ME: Can you feel the pain of the relationship just as it is now?

> WOMAN: Yes.

> ME: What are the actual sensations?

> WOMAN: Well, my chest aches a lot. Also my stomach feels tight as a snare drum. I've got the beginnings of a headache, too.

> ME: In the back of your neck and head?

> WOMAN: Yes.

(There are several different types of headaches; I wanted to find out quickly which type she had. If there's tension or pain in the neck and back of the head, it's likely to be the muscle-contraction variety, which is connected to the emotion of anger.)

ME: Of all those sensations, which one is strongest?

WOMAN: My chest.

ME: Rest your attention on your chest for ten seconds. Just feel what you feel there.

WOMAN (closes her eyes for ten seconds): Pressure and heaviness.

ME: Those sensations are in a place that usually is about sadness or longing. Can you feel what you're longing for?

WOMAN (beginning to sob): It's that special feeling we had when we were first together. Before we had kids, before the affairs, before the drinking started.

ME: Let your attention rest on those sensations till you can feel some space and flow around them.

WOMAN (pauses for ten to fifteen seconds): Okay.

ME: Now I want you to ask your body a question. Tune in and feel the pain of the relationship . . . then feel the creative possibilities of the relationship. Can you feel any creative possibilities in the relationship? Or has the pain destroyed all the creative possibilities?

WOMAN (pauses ten seconds): I don't feel any possibilities left.

I always accept the person's answer as is, without challenging it or asking if the person is sure. I know that she may feel differently tomorrow, but it's important to accept how she feels right now.

The Second Question

Now that she has assessed the ratio of pain to possibility, she is ready for the second of the two questions.

> ME: Okay, so now I have one more question for you to consider in your body. The question is: *Can you live with the consequences of breaking up right now?*
>
> WOMAN (pauses for ten seconds): I don't think so. Not right now. I don't have the energy to take him on as an adversary . . . not while I'm going to school part-time and trying to get my last teenager off to college. I just don't think I have the strength. I want to be realistic . . .
>
> ME: And that's perfectly appropriate. Right this moment, accept yourself just as you are. Relax into knowing this is an okay place to be.

I think it is equally important to accept her answer to the second question, knowing that the answer may change later. Reason and logic are powerful forces, but first we have to honor the wisdom of our bodies. If our logical mind is busily trying to persuade our body to leave or stay, it puts us in a frightful bind. Often we needlessly put our feelings and our logical mind in conflict, when only a warmhearted embrace of both will carry us through.

There are two Ten-Second Miracles here. The first miracle occurred when she tuned in to her body, feeling whether there was any possibility left amid the pain. Until that moment, I doubt that she had given herself those crucial few seconds of nonjudgmental attention that all of us deeply need. The second miracle occurred the moment she tuned in to find out if she could live with breaking up. It's important to know whether you are still open to the possibilities of the relationship or just marking time, waiting to get out. It is equally important to know if you have the strength and resources *right now* to make the break. Until your body gives you a clear signal one way or the other, you exist in a limbo state that eats up your energy. If you look the situation in the eye and accept where you stand, you reclaim the energy that the limbo state is eating up.

I've felt this shift many times in my own body, and indeed it is a miracle.

THE FIFTH MISTAKE

You've been wounded and don't know how to feel trust again.

I have a piece of radical advice for you: Never say "I'm sorry" to anyone you care about. This may sound bizarre, but I mean it and I'll tell you why. I've witnessed hundreds of people trying to apologize for something they've done. Most of them have first tried to do it with an "I'm sorry" or "I'm really, really sorry." They have often followed the "I'm sorry" with an explanation or justification of why they did whatever they did. Then they cap off the apology with a promise never to do it again.

Never once, in thirty years as a healing professional, have I seen "I'm sorry" or a promise to do better produce any long-term positive results. It's a Band-Aid that always comes loose, a salve that often makes the wound worse. There is a much better way to make amends, and it never takes longer than ten seconds. When you use the new way, organic resolution occurs. The result is much healthier than any apology could ever be.

Why Apologies Don't Work

There are two good reasons why apologies usually don't work.

First, an apology casts the apologizer in the role of perpetrator and the other person in the role of victim. It locks the situation into an unequal paradigm, robbing both people of the opportunity to take responsibility for their own end of the situation. In other words, if one person agrees that he or she is the perpetrator, that keeps the other person from seeing how he or she has contributed to the problem.

Second, apologies often paint over cracks in a relationship that should be explored in detail rather than covered up. The apology may provide a short-term solution, but the crack will often reappear later and be worse than before. If you say "I'm sorry," you stop the exploration just when it ought to be gaining momentum.

Making amends is an important part of life. When there's been a wound in a relationship, we need a ritual to put the issue away and move on. But it is important not to use apologies to obtain temporary relief at the expense of learning something important.

The Ten-Second Breakthrough

Instead of apologizing, make amends with the following steps:

1. Acknowledge what actually happened.

2. Make room for both people to air any feelings about the event.

3. Take personal responsibility for the event as it occurred.

4. Ask the question, What can we learn from this?

All of these are Ten-Second moves, and not one of them puts anybody in the victim position. They allow us to resolve the issue as equals.

As an example, let's say we had a lunch appointment for noon. I show up late, at 12:15. If I say "I'm sorry" and sit down, my apology identifies you as the victim of my lateness. An apology stops the learning process, and it keeps us from a genuine interaction. Let's do it another way:

I sit down.

ME: I realize we had an agreement to meet at noon and I'm here fifteen minutes late. I'm afraid you'll think I'm inconsiderate. I acknowledge breaking our agreement, and I regret any inconvenience I've caused you.

YOU: No big deal. I was worried I'd written down the time wrong. I've done that before. What happened?

ME: Traffic. Big snarl-up on the bridge . . . a truck tipped over and spilled cabbages everywhere.

YOU: I hate cabbage.

ME: Me too.

YOU: You have exquisite taste.

The key here is that neither of us had to make ourselves wrong in any way. I expressed a fear and a regret, and I acknowledged my responsibility without offering any excuses. I also made room for you to tell me any feelings or reactions you might have had. In this case, there probably isn't much I can learn from the experience except to give myself more time to get places.

The great advantage of making amends in this way is that it opens up possibilities for intimacy. You and I connected on a profound level: our mutual distaste for cabbage. Lifelong friendships have been founded on far less.

The Ten-Second Formula for Making Amends

Use the following script as an outline from which to improvise. You will touch on all the key items that an effective apology is based on, without having to label yourself as "sorry."

I want to acknowledge that I didn't keep our agreement to [be here on time]. I feel [regret, sadness, fear] about breaking our agreement. I'm open to listening to anything from you about it. I'd also like to discuss anything we need to do about it.

What creates conflict is failing to acknowledge the broken agreement and failing to air feelings about it. Many people are quick to apologize because they know it's a way to sweep feelings under the rug. In other words, they use apologies to avoid things that need to be faced squarely. Deal with the feelings straight on and you'll find that the flow of positive energy returns quickly.

THE SIXTH MISTAKE

*You procrastinate in communicating a
difficult feeling or truth.*

Avoiding difficult communications wastes a huge amount
of energy in close relationships. Avoiding saying the one
thing that must be said costs us intimacy and even physical
well-being. I'd like to share with you a painful personal example, to illustrate some of the problems that can befall us
when we put our energy into avoiding rather than facing
what needs to be said.

In my early thirties I was in a relationship with a lovely
woman whom I'll call Laura. After a while, I realized I didn't
have a long-term interest in her, but instead of making a
clean break, I continued seeing her sporadically. To my dis-
credit, I let her continue to believe I was committed to her.
Looking back with two decades' perspective, I think I did so
for three reasons: I enjoyed some of the physical comforts of
being with her, I didn't have anybody else, and I was afraid of
her reaction if I told her flat out that I was leaving. She had
a big issue about abandonment—"Please say you'll never

leave me" was one of her oft-used phrases—and the one time I'd started to tell her the truth, she'd become so upset that I chickened out.

A couple of months passed in this manner, and then I met another woman I was deeply attracted to. I started seeing the other woman, but I couldn't bring myself to tell Laura. I'll bet the thought *I've gotta tell her* flickered through my mind fifty times a day, but I didn't have the courage to do it.

Finally, after squandering all that energy on avoidance, I ended up doing it in just about the worst way possible. On a trip to a nearby state, I was driving alone in my car when I saw a telephone booth. I had a strong intuition to pull over and call Laura right then. I slowed down to do so, then my "weasel-self" won out and I stepped on the accelerator and sped down the road. An hour or so later, I started getting sick—really sick. It felt like some sort of rapid-onset flu—my nose streaming, my joints aching, my head pounding like a timpani. I remember having the thought that I'd never felt an illness come on so quickly in my life.

Then, a radical thought seized me. Was I making myself sick in punishment for not heeding my impulse to stop at that telephone booth? I waved off the thought with a "That's ridiculous." (This was in the days before it became common knowledge that our minds can affect our bodies.) I bought a box of tissues and a flu remedy and hit the road again.

Well, things went from bad to worse. Within hours, I could barely function. It had started pouring rain by then. Unbelievably, something went wrong with my windshield wipers, and in the act of fixing them I got soaking wet. Back in the car, I sat there for a while, shivering and hacking with streaming eyes and nose. Finally, I got the message.

It suddenly hit me that my life was going to continue to go like this until I reconciled the split in me. If I tried to live two lives, I wouldn't do either of them very well. As the Book of James says, "A double-minded man is unstable in all his ways." I drove to a phone booth and made the call.

After the usual "Hello" and "How are you?" I made my Ten-Second Communication.

"Laura, I'm feeling sick and scared to tell you this, and I'm feeling guilty I haven't told you before, but I'm very interested in another woman and I don't want to be lovers with you anymore."

I had steeled myself for a huge blowup, and the way she reacted was the last thing I expected. It seemed like a miracle, and still does twenty-five years later.

"Thank you," she said, starting to cry. "I think I knew it all along down inside. I just didn't want to face it, is all."

We talked calmly and straightforwardly for twenty minutes, then said "I love you" to each other and meant it. My "flu" disappeared from my body within hours.

There are two points I want to extract from that story. First and foremost, every moment we delay saying the thing that must be said comes with a cost. I'm convinced that delaying my Ten-Second Communication to Laura was what made me sick. I guess I was so thick in those days that it took a crisis to get through to me. I'm also convinced that delivering the essential communication was what caused the spontaneous remission of my illness.

The second point is that most of us are a lot more telepathic than we think. Laura picked up on my duplicity right away, but her trust of her intuition was so weak that she ignored it. I'm not saying that intuition is always correct—

quite often what seems like an intuitive flash is nothing more than a fear-thought in a pretty outfit. It took me years to learn to filter out the fears and projections that were flavoring my intuitions. Once I got clear intuition on the line, however, it became one of my best friends, and I predict it will become one of yours if you put your attention on it.

Over the years I have worked with many people to help them deliver essential communications.

Once I asked a couple—he a lawyer, she a librarian—if they had any secrets they had withheld from each other. Then I stood by in stunned surprise as they confessed to fourteen separate affairs, including one sexual experience she'd had two hours before their wedding fourteen years before. The liaison had been with the best man. Quite frankly, I expected disaster from this massive truth dump; instead, they came in for their next session with a moving recommitment to each other.

Another time, I listened to a kindly looking woman utter the phrase "I killed my mother." She meant it literally. She had helped her mother, her body riddled with cancer, swallow a bottle of sleeping pills. My client had carried the guilty memory of that moment with her for years. I watched it melt from her body when she faced and forgave her compassionate action.

From experiences like those, I have come to a conclusion: It is far better to say our truths than not to say them, and it's far better to say them quickly than to put them off. But our truth telling has to be done skillfully to have maximum healing benefits. I would like to give you a format I've found useful for helping people make difficult and essential communications. Perhaps not all these suggestions will apply to your situation; however, they are all "kitchen-tested" in the real world of relationship interaction. They are designed to help you avoid the major mistakes we tend to make under pressure.

Rule One

Take responsibility not only for speaking the difficult truth, but also for the way you want to be heard.

If you want to be listened to, be sure to pick a time when the other person can give full attention to what you're saying. It took me half my life to figure out this simple fact: Communication happens only when the other person understands what I'm saying. The best way to find out if the other person is willing to listen is also the simplest: Ask.

Be smart about the timing, too.

Don't make the big confession about your secret lover while your spouse is driving you down the freeway at seventy miles per hour. I wouldn't mention this example if I hadn't encountered it in a therapy session.

The Move: *"I have something I want to talk to you about. Is this a good time for you to listen? Are you willing to give it your full attention right now?"*

If yes, continue. If no, back off and do it another time.

Rule Two

If you don't already have a commitment to honesty and authenticity in the relationship, get one before speaking a difficult truth.

One of the first commitments my wife and I made to each other was to be absolutely honest with each other. We made an agreement to speak the truth and listen to the truth, no matter how inconvenient it might be or how much we might protest. That agreement has been possibly the most important conversation we've ever had. It has saved us many conversations such as,

"Did you really need to tell me that?"

"Why did you have to tell me that now?"

"Can't you see I'm busy?"

One of the main reasons people hide the truth from each other (or from themselves) is to protect an image of themselves or the relationship. If the reality of their feelings is in conflict with the image of how they're supposed to feel, often they sacrifice reality to protect the fantasy. That's a dangerous road to go down. Kathlyn and I decided to take a radical path: By agreeing that nothing—not even our image of ourselves or our marriage—was more important than saying or hearing the truth, we opened ourselves to painful feelings that many people stay closed to. By opening ourselves to reality, however—and by setting aside our image of ourselves— we have built a strong foundation that's only become more solid through nearly two decades.

The Move: *"I'd like a relationship with you where we are absolutely honest with each other, one where we are willing to speak the truth and hear it from each other. Would you be willing to commit to that with me?"*

If you get a yes, you are ready to do a quick soul search. Answer these questions honestly:

Are you interested in communicating clearly so that you can have a harmonious relationship?

OR

Are you trying to prove a point of some kind?

Many people are not really interested in communicating—they're interested in proving things such as:

You don't understand me.

Nothing I do works with you.

This relationship is doomed.

In other words, they are communicating with an agenda other than clarity, understanding, and harmony. After doing the following for a while myself, I began to ask my clients to do the same. I asked them to observe the intention behind every sentence they spoke. If you do this for a while, you will be amazed, as I was, how many things you say are not about producing harmony. I was humbled to discover that upward of half the words that came out of my mouth were serving agendas that were hidden even from myself. It took me about a year of observing my communication agendas before I could feel reasonably sure that most of my words were genuinely about communicating clearly.

The Move: *Take a deep breath and ask yourself a blunt question: Am I doing this to communicate or am I doing this to be right?*

If you can say honestly that you are there to communicate, *say the One-Breath statement that must be said.* You'll know you said it if you feel more organic good feeling after saying it. If you didn't say the thing that had to be said, you'll feel flat or dull or irritated or stuck. Then it's time to try again.

THE SEVENTH MISTAKE

You stagnate in an uncommitted relationship because you don't know how to make or ask for a commitment.

Without commitment, nothing is possible in relationships. As I said earlier in the book, all relationship problems are, at the core, commitment problems. A commitment issue—a broken commitment or one that never got made—lies under the pile of rubble in all relationship disasters. It all starts with commitment.

Hardly ever has there been a word more misunderstood. When most people hear *commitment*, they cringe from it or shoulder it like a burden. In some languages, the word for *commitment* also means burden, duty, and obligation.

Let's start fresh, with a brand-new understanding of what commitment really is:

When commitment really works, people never feel it as a burden or an obligation. It's not a yoke around our necks—it's the rock beneath our feet. It's not a gun to our heads—it's the energy source that's turned on by marshaling our resources toward a chosen vision.

When commitment really works, people feel it as an open space through which they can express their highest potential.

At our best, we feel commitment as a celebration that enlivens every moment. Rather than collapsing under the burden of duty, people feel the lightness of spirit that comes from having all the cells of their bodies aligned behind a worthy goal.

The Secrets

There are three secrets to getting commitment. All are incredibly simple, yet many people find them impossible to master. To get commitment from other people, you must:

1. Be committed yourself, so that your example inspires commitment in the other person.

2. Ask for what you want directly.

3. Watch the other person's reaction and speak to it.

Here's how it works.

Suppose you have been dating someone for a year and want to get married. Your first move is to make sure you're ready to make a commitment yourself. If you are, then you need to make yourself an open space to receive commitment. In other words, you need to make yourself "committable to." This might mean letting go of any and all self-imposed barriers, such as your limiting beliefs. Many people, for example, carry a limiting belief that says, "I'm not worth committing to. I wouldn't want to be committed to anybody who'd want to be committed to a person like me." This belief is more effective than skunk spray at keeping people from committing to you.

The first move, then, is to make sure you are completely willing to be in a committed relationship. Muster the courage to look at the situation directly: "The evidence that I'm not in a committed relationship tells me I'm not open to it in some way I don't understand. I'm willing to find out what I'm doing or thinking or believing that's keeping me from being in a committed relationship." Magic happens when you find the courage to face yourself honestly like that. It's been my privilege to be with many people as they entertained that thought for the first time, and I can guarantee you that it works magic.

After you drop your internal barriers to commitment, then you encounter the second hurdle: asking. We all know how hard that is. I remember a miserably hot Sunday afternoon as a kid, when we rode around lost for hours because my Uncle Bob would not stop to ask for directions. The more frustrated my Aunt Audrey and we kids became, the more Uncle Bob dug in his heels. To him, asking directions was an admission of unmanliness, tantamount to a matador's excusing himself from the bullring because of a dropped hankie. How simple it would have been to pull over to a gas station and ask, "Where is the back road to the county fairgrounds?" Little did he know that his pigheadedness would one day earn him an unflattering bit part in a relationship book!

Back to our example: Suppose you are able to open yourself to commitment, to make yourself worth committing to. Suppose also you are willing to ask for what you want. You take a deep breath and say, "I want a committed relationship with you that results in marriage." The next ten seconds after you ask will tell you what you really need to know.

In those ten seconds the other person will reveal if there are any barriers to matching your commitment. Your job is to speak to what you see, not to interpret. In fact, if you refrain from interpretation, you will see miracles happen.

Here's what I mean, drawn from a situation I saw in my office:

YOU: I want a committed relationship that leads to marriage within the year.

YOUR PARTNER (crosses arms, frowns, scratches head): Well, that sounds like a plan.

YOU: I notice you crossed your arms and frowned when I said what I wanted. I notice you didn't say yes or no.

Your partner has engaged in a defensive move, but that doesn't mean you have to! If you will simply acknowledge the defensive move—not interpret it—you will see magic unfold very quickly. Very few people get to see that magic because they jump into a defensive posture themselves, a posture that is based on interpretation.

Here's the way it often goes when people jump into interpretation:

YOU: I want a committed relationship . . .

PARTNER (crosses arms . . .): Well, that sounds like a plan.

YOU: Look at you! You've never committed to anything in your whole sorry life. Here you are, getting the chance to have a wonderful person like me, and you stall around.

If we can avoid interpretation in the crucial ten-second window after the other's reaction, miracles can happen. Let's go further with the example:

PARTNER (crosses arms . . .): Well, that sounds like a plan.

YOU: I notice you crossed your arms and frowned when I said what I wanted. I notice you didn't say yes or no.

PARTNER (silence for several seconds): I'm scared.

YOU: Me too. What are you scared of?

PARTNER: Getting hurt again.

YOU: Ah. Me too. But I figure if I don't risk commitment again, I'll stay boxed in forever.

PARTNER: You're right. Let's go for it.

By refraining from interpretation—by speaking to what's real (the crossed arms, the frown)—you create an open space in which miracles can appear. If you jump into your interpretation, you imprint the open space with your old patterns. The space is filled, the window closes, and the merry-go-round continues. If you will risk being the miracle worker, the one who opens the space rather than dumps old patterns into it, you will engineer one miracle after another.

BREAKTHROUGH SOLUTIONS FOR PROBLEMS OF LONG-TERM RELATIONSHIPS

PART THREE

THE FOURTH MIRACLE

*Stopping the Past from Intruding
on the Present*

For many of us, the past seems ominous and vast and gaining on us by the minute. We all have histories of painful losses of one kind or another. Sometimes it's hard to believe we will ever escape the burden of the past. Many of us are tucked into a permanent cringe from the past—we think it's bigger than we are and that we're its victims. I know all this because I've felt it myself. But I discovered a secret that changed my life. You may have a hard time believing this secret, but if you embrace it, your life will change in the blink of an eye.

The secret: The past does not exist.

There is no such thing. The past is a lie.

There is something true about the past, though, and it is profoundly true. Once you understand it thoroughly, pain begins to melt from your body.

What is true about the past is that we bring it to life in our bodies. The past lives in the present when we resist the emotions we haven't accepted from the past. When you shrink from a feeling triggered by a long-ago event, you create the past in your body right now. The past is a lie, but that fist in your chest is true. Forget the past—don't think about it again—but put your attention on what is real in your body. The painful legacy of past wounds will start to melt the moment you face and feel what's real.

There is a reason the past seems bigger than we are. It's because we are holding it at arm's length. The energy it takes to mount that resistance saps our strength. We deflate the past quickly the moment we face it squarely and fully feel its leftover emotions. Once we face our feelings squarely and resonate with them thoroughly, we cease to be concerned with the past. We often stall for years before facing and resonating with some feeling from the past, but once we make the move, we are healed virtually instantly. I've never seen it take even ten seconds.

The Fourth Miracle Rule

The Rule: *The moment you face the feelings of your past, you release the effects of the past from your body and mind.*

Feel what's real and you heal.

For example, you may feel wounded because a true love rejected you fifteen years ago. To heal this wound, you must face what happened and *everything you feel about it.* In my office, I've been present to people facing this moment hundreds of times, and that's why I can give you the wonderful news that it takes only a few seconds—if you are willing to face the issue unflinchingly.

Look in the three core zones of your body for what you need to feel. When you face an event in your past, the zone of your body that's most affected will freeze up, rev up, or tense up. When you face your beloved's rejection of you, you will probably feel your throat constrict or your chest clench. You may feel the hackle of anger begin to rise, or a queasy tickle of fear in your stomach. When you face the issue unflinchingly, you will invite the reality of it into your body awareness. This is a good thing. You have to be aware of it before you can release it.

Facing and feeling only take a few seconds. Just keep your attention on the real sensations of the past—the grip of longing or the tension of anger—for long enough to feel the sensations start to shift. And the sensations begin to shift with ten seconds of focus.

The Key Question

Right now, answer a Key Question:

What are you carrying from the past that you have not faced squarely?

If you will turn to face it for ten seconds, you will be free of it. The moment you fully face what you're carrying, you're free of its burden. If an actual gorilla is pursuing you down the street, facing it fully may help, but it won't make you free of it. The past is different from an actual gorilla. The past is a gorilla that lives only between your ears. The moment you take full, healthy responsibility—right now—for something that happened in your past, it begins to release from your body—right now. Until you claim full responsibility for it, it continues to run, and often ruin, your life.

Here's an example. I was driven by the issue of abandonment for much of my early relationship life. For a long time I didn't know I had an unconscious problem with abandonment. I just thought I had bad luck with women leaving me. Eventually, I built a hard shell—"I won't get close to people"—around the tender issue of abandonment. It's probably the only solution my unconscious mind could come up with to keep me from being hurt. My unconscious mind probably reasoned, If I don't ever get close to people, nobody will ever leave me.

Finally, I had a big wake-up in my early thirties. I realized that I kept pushing women away so they wouldn't leave me. By holding them at a distance, I got to stay in control. One day I saw that the whole thing was connected to the departure of my mother when I was a baby. My survival mind must have taken a fix on this event, and then I replayed it over and over as a teen and young adult. That was the way I thought life was supposed to be: You get close to people and then they leave you.

Here's the amazing part: This issue didn't shift until I took responsibility for it in the present. Even though I didn't understand all the details, I jumped in and said, "I cause the lack of intimacy in my life." I claimed responsibility for as many of the details as I could:

"I cause women to leave me."

"I cause my emotional distance."

"I cause my fear of abandonment."

As I did this, the fear melted out of my body. My relationship life turned around completely. The issue of abandonment and fear of intimacy quickly disappeared. There was one immediate benefit: Before I reached this resolution, I'd always tended to go on eating binges when someone I was close to went out of town, even on an overnight trip. Suddenly this tendency disappeared, with other changes soon to follow.

Here's the paradox we face: How can we claim responsibility for something we didn't cause in the first place? After all, I didn't cause the departure of my mother, nor did you cause your father to drink or your brother to molest you or any one of the hundreds of events that shape our lives before we can think straight. There is a logical answer for this paradox, which I'll get to in a moment. But the logic of it all, no matter how interesting, is also totally irrelevant.

The move that heals you is to claim responsibility for any relationship issue for *no reason other than the sheer joy and power of doing so.* Notice I did not say to blame yourself or to burden yourself with responsibility for an issue. True responsibility is taken as a celebration of freedom, not as blame or a burden.

Here's where the logical answer to the paradox fits in. Even though you probably weren't the cause of the original event, you are the cause of keeping it going in your life now. Again, this is irrelevant, because your life doesn't change until you claim responsibility for it yourself. Even though a judge and jury may tell criminals that they are responsible for their crimes, their lives won't change until they claim responsibility themselves. Having worked in prisons earlier in my career, I can tell you that the first thing you learn is that almost all inmates think they're there by mistake! Very few take any responsibility for being in prison. Nearly all of them have an incredible story about why they're there. No matter what the details are, the punch line of the story is the same. The punch line is that they've been wronged, that even though they may have stuck up the liquor store and killed the clerk and run over somebody trying to escape, it was actually somebody else's fault. Of course, that way of thinking is why they're in prison. It's also why we're in whatever prison we happen to be in.

The way out is simple: Claim responsibility for anything that troubles you. Claim it for no good reason. Claim it without waiting for anything else to happen before you claim it. As the shoe ad says, just *do* it:

"I cause my lack of fulfillment in my marriage."

"I cause my depression."

"I cause my aloneness."

"I cause my weight problem."

"I cause my allergies."

Notice that these statements can be made in less than ten seconds—most of them in three or four seconds. I've been privileged to hear real people speak these sentences, and I've been deeply moved to watch their lives change rapidly in every case. In each case, the person claimed responsibility— for no reason other than the pure exhilaration of it—for something he or she had complained about for years. In each case, the issue disappeared, sometimes so fast that neither of us could believe it.

I'll never forget the first time I saw this miracle at work. When I give you the details, I think you'll see why it's so memorable. In 1974 I was just starting my career as a professor in the counseling psychology department at the University of Colorado. One of my graduate students asked me if he could talk to me about an issue that was, in his words, "driving me to distraction." We sat down in the student lounge over a cup of coffee for what I thought was going to be a chat about some bureaucratic snafu. It turned out, though, that he was obsessing about a personal issue, his girlfriend's nose.

He told me that he hated the shape of his girlfriend's nose, that he'd hated it ever since they met, and that he had recently been thinking about it night and day. Because of his earnest expression I was able to suppress a strong urge to say, "You've got to be kidding!" As it happened, I knew his girlfriend well because she was a student in two of my classes, including the one he was in. Indeed, I could see her sitting at a table not fifty feet from where he and I were talking. There was nothing out of the ordinary about the shape of her nose, as far as I could tell.

I asked, "Want to solve this problem right this minute?" He gratefully nodded yes.

"It doesn't have anything to do with her nose. Forget her nose. Take responsibility for why *you* are obsessing about this right now. What does this have to do with *you!*"

It's one of the few times in my life I've actually seen someone's jaw drop.

He said, "I hate my nose. I've always hated my nose. I never thought about it until this minute."

"What about your nose do you hate?"

He smiled sheepishly. "The shape of it." I studied his nose. It *did* have a slight crook to it, though it wasn't by any means prominent.

"Okay," I said. "Welcome to the club. I'm not too crazy about my nose, either. I've always thought mine's too big. Any other reason why you'd be finding fault with her right now?"

He ducked his head and whispered, "She wants to get married. I think I'm drumming up reasons not to do that."

"How about claiming responsibility for not wanting to get married? It'd take the pressure off her nose."

He grinned and stood up. "Thanks."

He sidled up to me after class the next week and told me the nose obsession had ceased completely. He also said they'd had a good laugh when he'd recounted our conversation to her. And what about the dreaded moment when he told her he didn't want to get married? She'd greeted this with, "You think I didn't know that?" All was swell again and remained so, at least until semester's end when I lost touch with them.

And now let's turn to feelings.

What really troubles us is when feelings from the past intrude on the present. You and your lover are enjoying dinner in a nice restaurant one moment and the next moment some old feeling from long ago washes over you. Suddenly you are embroiled in a conflict that is just like one from an hour ago or a decade ago. Your body is planted in the present, but everything else about you is caught up in an old drama from the past.

And most of the time, the troublesome intruder from the past is a feeling—anger, sadness, fear. Suddenly, there it is in your body. Now what?

A Universal Problem with Feelings

People are afraid of some feelings and addicted to others. They are afraid of their own feelings and the feelings of others. Time and again, I see the same costly mistake being made when the problem could be handled in less than ten seconds.

Here's the mistake: A feeling comes up that needs to be addressed. Instead of facing it directly, the person ignores it, minimizes it, changes the subject, or tries to fix it. By shrinking from feelings, we break one of the fundamental rules of life, which is . . .

The Feeling Rule

WHEN FEELINGS COME UP, FACE THEM DIRECTLY BUT DON'T TRY TO *DO* ANYTHING WITH THEM. PARTICULARLY, NEVER TRY TO FIX THEM OR TALK ANYONE OUT OF THEM. ANYONE INCLUDES YOURSELF.

ALWAYS ACKNOWLEDGE YOUR FEELINGS TO *YOURSELF*, BUT *SPEAK* THEM ONLY TO PEOPLE YOU WANT TO BE CLOSER TO.

Look at a violation of the Feeling Rule, and ask yourself how many times the same thing has happened in your life:

YOU: I'm afraid of flunking the real estate exam tomorrow.

CO-WORKER: Oh, you'll do fine.

The person may mean well by reassuring you. But sweeping a feeling under the rug always has a negative effect on relationships. Hundreds of times on videotapes I've seen this moment occur, and it reliably leads to distance and destruction in the relationship. Feelings can't be ignored, nor can they be fixed—they simply must be honored, listened to, breathed with. In short, *feelings must be given a few seconds of breathing space.* That's all they usually need to begin resolving themselves.

You don't have to *do* anything with feelings. You couldn't

anyway. Feelings are like rainstorms—they have a beginning, a middle, and an end. Many people ignore feelings because they fear that if they acknowledge them, they will have to do something with them. We erroneously think that if we feel our sadness we'll be stuck with it forever, or if we acknowledge our anger it means there is something wrong with us.

RELATIONSHIPS GROW OR ERODE ACCORDING TO HOW YOU HANDLE THE FEELING MOMENT.

Look at another violation of the Feeling Rule, followed by the same example in which the rule is applied correctly.

YOU: Hi, John. How are you today?

CO-WORKER: Tired. I've been up since 3:00 A.M. with our baby. She's teething.

YOU: How 'bout a cup of coffee to wake you up?

Although offering coffee to a tired person might seem compassionate, it is an unwise move unless you speak directly to the feeling first. Here's how you would do that:

CO-WORKER: Tired. I've been up since 3:00A.M. . . .

YOU: That must be exhausting. And frustrating.

CO-WORKER: Yeah, it's really frustrating.

YOU: Is there any way I can help?

You will find that most people do not take you up on your offer of help. They need to have their feelings acknowledged. It feels good to them to be offered a compassionate ear and a helping hand, even if they don't actually want you to help in a tangible way. Usually, ten seconds of being with people's feelings is about all that's required. In the example above, the entire move took only a few seconds. It is always time well spent. From the evidence on the videotapes, it reliably works miracles. All you need to do is face a feeling directly, and you can leave it behind. If you don't speak to it, it usually comes back to haunt you later.

Be Vigilant About Four Feelings

There are only four feelings that play a major role in everyday communication: longing, fear, anger, and sadness. Get good at handling the moments when these occur, and your life changes dramatically.

Sexual feelings are a special case. Although it is often unwise to speak directly about a sexual feeling out loud, you must always speak to it telepathically. Acknowledge it in yourself or the other person. Sexual feelings are best handled by resonating with them. I counseled a young man who had developed a powerful sexual attraction to a woman at work. Not only was she his supervisor, she was married and eight years his senior. There were plenty of good reasons not to address the issue directly with her.

First, I invited him to do the First Miracle Move with his sexual feelings:

"Focus your nonjudgmental attention on the sensations of sexual attraction, as you can feel them right now in your body."

"They're everywhere!" he exclaimed.

"Stay with them, wherever they are," I replied.

After focusing on the feelings for a few seconds, he realized they were not actually everywhere. Rather, they were streaming pleasant sensations from his belly down to his knees. He relaxed visibly once he localized his feelings in his body. That often happens—before we pin down our feelings in a specific body location, they feel huge and boundless and universal. Once we've pinned them down and resonated with them, they feel manageable and safer to deal with.

After a few minutes another key factor emerged: His supervisor was a lot like his older sister. She was tall and brunette and had a critical edge to her. He said all these characteristics reminded him of his sister. Now we entered the territory of the taboo. He needed to give himself permission to resonate with sexual feelings toward his sister. These were feelings he had kept hidden for more than a decade. The Miracle worked again, though. By letting himself resonate with those long-sealed-away feelings, he relaxed so much that he fell asleep in his chair. I had to wake him after a few moments, because I had another appointment. The Miracle continued to work: Not only did he lose sexual interest in his supervisor overnight, he also developed a closer tie with his sister and her husband and children.

The bottom line: Resonating with your feelings is always a good move. Speaking them out loud is not always a good move. In fact, be selective about speaking out loud about your feelings. Take time before speaking about your feelings to ask yourself: "Is this person likely to give my feelings a good reception?" I counsel my clients to make sure they have at least three friends who are completely safe to talk to about

anything, and who feel the same about them. Most of us
don't need twenty such friends, but we do need a few. If you
have that friendship network already established, congratula-
tions. If not, put it on your to-do list.

How To

*Resonating with a feeling is simple: Pause and feel the
sensations in your body through three deep breaths.
That's usually enough to keep your feelings from turning
into distress symptoms such as headaches and digestive
upsets.*

*If you're feeling anger, resonate with the tension in your
back, your shoulders, your jaws.*

*If you're feeling sadness or longing, resonate with the
lump in your throat, the clench in your chest, the tears in
your eyes.*

*If you're feeling scared, resonate with the antsy, queasy
butterflies and the tight fist in your stomach.*

Usually the feeling moment passes right by because we
don't know what to do about it. Once you focus on it, you'll
realize that you have felt it often, both when you were alone
and when you were in a relationship.

Alone and Together

There are two types of feeling moments we need to learn
how to handle: when we are by ourselves and when we are
around other people.

The First Feeling Moment

First, let's look at how the feeling moment occurs when no one else is around.

The Situation

You are sitting by yourself, at home or in your office. A while ago, you were with someone or talking to someone, but now you are by yourself. Suddenly you realize you feel a little "off." There is an unsettled, off-center feeling of tension in your body.

You are experiencing a feeling moment. You are in the grip of a feeling that needs to be explored. *What you do in the next ten seconds could change your life, or even destroy it.* I used to raid the refrigerator when I was in the grip of this feeling moment. I can remember being home alone after school when I was a kid. The lonely feeling would build and build until I couldn't stand it, and then I would stuff myself to make it go away. It never did. It just receded into the background, behind the stuffed sensation.

The Second Feeling Moment

Another important feeling moment happens when other people are around.

The Situation

You are talking to someone who is important in your life. You sense a tension between the two of you, so you ask, "What's going on? What are you feeling?" The other person says, "Nothing." At the moment you hear this, though, you notice his or her eyes slide off to one side. Something doesn't feel quite right inside you.

This is a feeling moment. An important emotion is present but is not being acknowledged or spoken. The other person is feeling something and not saying it, and you are feeling something and not saying it. You have ten seconds in which to bring your feelings into the light. If you can do this, your intimacy with the person will grow. If not, distance grows. If an important feeling is not faced directly, it becomes a potentially destructive force in the relationship.

If you learn to handle feeling moments correctly, you will open the flow of well-being inside yourself and the flow of love in your relationships. Feeling moments are crucial to your happiness and even to your physical health.

Those are strong words—can they be true?

Yes, but do not take my word for it. You can check out the truth inside your own body and mind. Return now to the situations we were discussing, and I'll show you how to check out the truth for yourself.

In both situations, that slightly off-center feeling is what I call a *flag*. It is like a flag waving at you, trying to get your attention. The deeper part of your mind and body is communicating with you the only way it can. The deeper part of your body and mind developed millions of years before your thinking mind came into being. When this deeper part communicates with you, it communicates in primitive language like signals and hunches.

What is the flag trying to tell you? The message is this: RIGHT NOW YOU ARE EXPERIENCING AN IMPORTANT FEELING. IT CONTAINS CRUCIAL INFORMATION FOR YOU.

Your body is registering that slightly agitated, off-center sensation until you take ten seconds to listen to your body. If you don't stop and listen to what your body is trying to tell you, you will feel unhappy and symptoms will start to appear.

You may be wondering: Aren't there a lot of feelings? How do I know which one to look and listen for? The answer is that there are only five crucial ones, which I'll list for you in a moment. Later I'll describe for you the precise sensations that will tell you which one has a grip on you at the moment. I'll begin with the four that cause the most problems if we don't learn to listen to them. They are all natural and normal and have been with us for thousands of years. Don't waste your time wondering if you have a right to feel any of these feelings or whether it's fitting or proper. When they're there, they're there. That's all we need to know for now. Focus your attention on learning to feel them when you're feeling them. The person who ignores them is in exactly the same position in life as a person driving on the freeway blindfolded.

By far, THE MOST COMMON FEELING WE IGNORE IS LONGING.

The second is ANGER.

The third is FEAR.

The fourth is SADNESS, and last is SEXUAL ATTRACTION.

You might think sexual attraction would be higher on the list, but it is not. Let's begin with the one that most of us feel most of the time ... *longing.*

How You Know When You're Longing

The main sensation of longing—how you know you are feeling it—is a tension in your chest. Years ago one of my clients called it "the fist in my heart," and I have never heard a better description. When you're longing, you feel an uncomfortable tightness around your heart and lungs. When you are in longing, you will also notice that your breathing is more up in your chest instead of down in your belly (although this is also true of some of the other feelings). Many people seek quick fixes to relax the fist in the chest—distractions such as alcohol, cigarettes, and food. It will tighten again, though, until you learn to deal with the real issue behind the fist. That's where Ten-Second Miracles become very important.

There is a milder sensation of longing that many of us feel much of the time. It's that slightly off-center feeling that I used in the two earlier examples. I called the "off" feeling a *flag*, because it is trying to get your attention. My research indicates that the "off" feeling is really a mild form of longing, the same feeling that would grip your chest in tension if it were stronger. The mild feeling has a key purpose: to bring our attention to some incompletion we need to handle. When we leave undone something important, our bodies go into a mild form of longing until we do it. We are longing for union with ourselves, and the only way to get reconnected is by handling the incompletion.

When the grip of longing is stronger, we are yearning for an important love connection. We are longing to connect with another person in such a way that we can feel a flow of love in ourselves and back and forth between us. If we don't have that connection, most likely we are longing for it. Even if we have a flowing love connection, often we feel longing when we're out of the person's field. When there is a strain in a relationship, the longing grows intense.

We also long for other things. Most of us desperately long to fulfill our creative potential. As I travel the world, I see millions of people unable or unwilling to take on the risky business of expressing creativity. To keep their minds off the longing they feel, they engage in a vast array of distractions, none of which ever works and most of which have dangerous side effects.

At one of my European seminars, I worked with a couple who had been fighting for months over seemingly trivial things like what kind of cheeses to buy. They even got into an argument during one of the lunch breaks—an argument about the type of salad dressing she'd brought from home. It was clear to everyone but them that the real issues had nothing to do with cheese or salad dressing. They volunteered to come into the center of the circle for a demonstration.

Within five minutes, the real issue emerged:

ME: What would you two be doing with all the energy that's being wasted on these cheese battles?

HANS: I don't understand.

I happened to know that Hans collected antique sports cars, so I tried an automotive metaphor.

ME: Well, let's say you've been burning ten gallons of gas a week keeping these arguments going. Where would you go with this fuel if you weren't wasting it keeping the argument revved up?

PETRA (breaking into laughter): You found the way to his heart.

HANS: I see. I am not working right now—in my art, I mean.

PETRA (soberly): Neither am I.

ME: Could that be it?

HANS: I am creating struggles because I am not being creative.

PETRA: That's it, isn't it?

ME: What would you be doing with all that energy?

PETRA: Making a film, composing a score.

HANS: Ja. We are idle right now. We have not had a film project in eight months. I am growing worried.

PETRA: And taking it out on each other.

Then these two talented people made a courageous decision right in front of the group.

ME: Would you drop all this fighting and put your attention on how you could be allies in creating a project to work on?

HANS: I would. (He smiles and sticks out his hand. They shake formally, and the group roars with laughter.)

PETRA: Okay. (After they shake hands, she throws her arms around him and the group cheers.)

We go into longing when we are cut off from someone or something important. Since we live inside our bodies, where our feelings also live, we often feel estranged from our very selves when we cannot feel deeply. When we are cut off from our feelings, this disconnection makes us ill at ease. It is a problem that most of us struggle with every day.

Bodies Thrive on Feeling

Our bodies love to feel deeply. When we live mainly in the arid world of concepts, we maintain a deep longing for immersion in the nurturing sea of feeling. There is nothing wrong with concepts—where would we be without them? It's just that we often wander around in them so long we become thirsty for experience. The concept of "water" is fine, but it is not wet. Human beings have been tossing concepts around for a relatively short time—in evolutionary terms, only for the blink of an eye. But feelings have been with us for a long, long time.

We are well wired for feeling. Long before we developed clarity of thinking, we were deeply immersed in feeling. Even our brains are more wired for feeling than for thinking. You've probably held a grapefruit in your hand. A good-sized grapefruit is about as large as our brains. Now compare the juicy part of the grapefruit to the rind. That's how big the feeling part of the brain is, compared to the thinking part.

The feeling and thinking parts of our minds yearn to be deeply connected with each other. We are at our best when we feel a rich interplay between thinking and feeling. We get out of harmony when there's a feeling inside that we haven't given ourselves conscious permission to feel. Then, the deeper part of us has to communicate by waving flags at us until we get the message. Without a harmony between thinking and feeling, we are like a grapefruit that has a six-inch gap between the juicy part and the rind. Nature didn't design it that way.

Feelings Connect Us with Other People

Our bodies yearn to connect with other people. We thrive on the feeling of unity flowing between us and others, and when it's not there, we long for it. Connection with others is so important that our bodies send up flags when something has broken the flow of unity. When we're hungry for connection, first we feel tension, then we feel pain. The tension and pain goad us to seek connection, but we don't have to wait until we're tight and hurting. The best medicine is preventive: We can prevent the tension and pain of disconnection by learning what breaks the flow between us and others. The flow is broken the moment we hide our feelings from each other.

Throughout our day we have flickers of feeling that don't come in loud and clear enough to get our full attention. Flickers of feeling often happen when we're busy doing something else—perhaps driving down a crowded highway. Although we may not notice the flicker consciously, part of us is listening intently. That part—our million-year-old survival brain—got us where we are today by being very good at noticing tiny shifts of emotion. In the old days, before the discovery of fire, shelter, and clothing, we lived in groups and slept huddled together for safety and warmth. It was to everyone's advantage to be highly attuned to sounds like distant coughs and rustles. Those who woke up first got to live and breed another day. Nowhere was the old saying "You snooze, you lose" more apt than in our primitive lives in the jungle and on the savanna.

We are a great deal more sensitive to feelings than we give ourselves credit for. It's just that until recently we haven't known what to do about them when they occur. So we learn to hide them. When you're sitting in front of your boss, feeling angry and scared, it's not considered appropriate to jump up and run when he starts criticizing your work.

Now that we've tuned in to longing, the next feeling we need to consider is . . . *anger*.

The anger zone in the human body corresponds to where the hackles are on an animal. When we feel angry, there is a tightening of muscles between the shoulder blades that extends into the neck and shoulders. Jaws also tighten. The place to focus on, though, is between your shoulder blades and up into your neck and shoulders—that's where you can pick up the early sensations of anger. Most of us feel flickers of it hourly, and our job is to know that we're angry when we're feeling it. If you don't notice when you're angry, you will get secondary symptoms of anger such as headaches and back pain.

What Triggers Anger

The trigger for anger is trespass or an unfair violation of boundaries. Don't waste time worrying about whether your anger is justified—simply put your attention on whether you feel it. If you're angry, you feel trespassed against or your boundaries feel violated. Sometimes there is a real-time, right-now trespass going on. Sometimes there is a relatively innocent situation in which you are perceiving trespass based on some past experience. If you have been trespassed on earlier in your life (and who hasn't?), you will sometimes be a trespass waiting to happen. In either case, your Miracle Move will be the same. Later, in a reflective mode with your journal or a glass of wine at hand, you can wonder about the source of your chronic stance of expecting trespass.

Some of us are extreme cases—deep anger is locked in as a chronic way of being. Many of the angriest people I've worked

with do not think of themselves as angry at all. You've probably met chronically angry people. You're probably not one of
them, because they usually don't read books like this. It's easy
to spot chronically angry people: They are the only people
who deny it angrily when people point out that they're angry.
In one memorable case, one of my medical colleagues recommended that a patient with chronic headaches get some psy-
chotherapy to work on reducing his chronic anger. The man,
a strapping six-foot-four 250-pounder, came out of his chair
and pinned my colleague to the wall.

"Are you suggesting that I'm an angry person?" he roared.

My colleague took a few breaths and said, "I'm scared of
you right now. Your anger is scaring me."

The man deflated like a punctured balloon.

"What do you mean?" he asked.

"Well," my colleague said, "you've got me backed up
against the wall and you were yelling at me. You resent my
calling attention to your anger, but who else but a very angry
person would be acting like you're acting."

A scene like this would be comical if it weren't so destructive to the person, and to those around him. The man was
using so much energy defending himself against his anger
that he had no control over it.

Breaking Through the Defensive Barrier

Most of us are not quite as defensive as the man in my
example, but just about all of us have some tendencies in that
direction. I know I still do, even after thirty years of working
on letting go of being defensive. Defensiveness is the main

barrier we must overcome in learning to handle the feeling moments of our lives. When we notice that off-center feeling in ourselves, it is defensiveness that has us reach for a cigarette or a snack instead of pausing to tune in to our bodies for a moment. When someone who cares about you asks, "What are you feeling right now?" you have a ten-second window of intimacy to *look and see and report*. If you get defensive in this window, you create trouble immediately in the relationship.

Let's take a look at some of the main defensive moves I see or hear reported in my office.

Defensive Move Number 1: The Wrong-Time Defense

WIFE: What are you feeling right now?

HUSBAND: Can't you see I'm busy right now? Can we talk about feelings some other time?

Notice that the same amount of time and energy put into defending could be put into a simple answer: "I'm feeling rushed and tired and grumpy."

Defensive Move Number 2: The Persecuted-Victim Defense

PERSON A: What are you feeling right now?

PERSON B: There you go picking on me again. Why are you always so fixated on feelings? Can't you just enjoy life for a little while without worrying about feelings?

Defensive Move Number 3: The Ignorance Defense

ME: What are you feeling right now?

CLIENT: I don't know.

Defensive Move Number 4: The Offensive Defense

"What are you feeling right now?"

"THAT'S IT! I'VE HAD IT WITH ALL THAT FEELING CRAP. IF YOU
    WEREN'T SO CONCERNED WITH FEELINGS, MAYBE YOU'D BE
    ABLE TO USE A LITTLE LOGIC NOW AND THEN."

Contrast these defensive moves with a healthy alternative. Instead of getting defensive in the ten-second window, we could learn to make two Miracle Moves: We could tune in to our authentic feelings, and we could report what we discover to the best of our ability.

Here's an example of a couple who were learning the value of undefended communication. This interchange took less than a minute, but it set a tone for the future of their relationship:

ME: Harriet, tune in to what's going on in your belly right now. You look really tense.

HARRIET: I'm scared. Scared as hell.

ME: Would you tell Larry directly?

LARRY (starts coughing furiously): Sorry.

ME: What's that cough covering up, Larry?

LARRY: I think I'm afraid of what she's going to say.

HARRIET: It's not really anything that bad. Really.

ME: Take a breath and say it in one breath.

HARRIET: I want to adopt a child.

LARRY: Jesus! Are you—

HARRIET: Wait, hear me out.

ME: Take a few breaths, Larry, and feel what you're feeling while you listen to her. You don't have to agree . . . just listen.

HARRIET: I'm 43. I'm a good teacher, but I'm never going to be a great one. What I really want to do is take time off and raise a child.

LARRY: When did you decide all this?

HARRIET: It's been bubbling around in the back of my mind for a long time.

LARRY: And you haven't said a word . . .

HARRIET: Well, I'm saying it now.

There were many negotiations over the next three sessions, but they were all worthwhile. The payoff for me was getting to see the radiant look on Larry's face as he held the Korean girl they'd flown to Asia to bring home.

LARRY: Do you believe I ever resisted this idea?

ME: People change, Larry, and you're going to be a great dad.

When you speak the truth of what you are feeling from an attitude of wonder and discovery, you create flow in your relationships. Truth spoken from wonder increases flow. Flow is strangled when you speak arguable things like opinions, and is cut off even more as you justify and explain those opinions.

Before I show you why this is so, we need to answer a fundamental question.

A Key Question: What Is *Flow?*

The feeling of flow is important to life and love. When you feel a sense of flow inside your body and mind, all is well. When there is flow between you and another person, all is well between you. But what exactly is flow? Take a moment now to focus on what it actually feels like in your body.

For many years, I have used the feeling of flow inside myself as my main barometer of health and well-being. My wife and I use the feeling of flowing connection as the main barometer of how our relationship is going. I have also worked to get a flow moving between people in more than three thousand relationship sessions. Based on those experiences, here is how I define flow. Flow is a sensation made up of three elements: movement, play, and space. Flow is the moving sensation of spaciousness and play. Take away movement and you have no flow. Take away the spacious feeling and you have no flow. Take away play and you definitely have no flow. When all three elements are present, in our bodies and in our relationships, we are flowing with life and love.

To feel what I mean, join me in an experiment.

The best place to begin is where you are right now. At this moment I'm in my living room in Montecito early on a Saturday morning. Soft music is playing in the room, and the dominant sound I can hear is the bubbling of the fountain in my garden. As I scan my body with my awareness, I notice a sensation of constriction in my left ankle. It feels stiff as a board, as if nothing is moving inside. Technically, of course, I know that lots of things are going on inside my ankle, but what's missing is the *sensation of easeful play*. I shift my awareness to my right ankle, and a world of difference opens up. My right ankle feels alive in the same place that my left ankle feels slightly deadened.

Scan your body and see if you can find a place that isn't flowing. Check your shoulders and neck—we often lose a sense of flow in those places. Feel the center of your body. Give your attention to any area where you find a lack of flow.

As I give my attention over to my lively right ankle, I notice an even subtler difference. Not only is there a felt sensation of easeful play, compared with the wooden feeling of my left ankle, but my right ankle feels more spacious, as if there is more room in it. I shift awareness back to my left ankle, and I notice I must focus more intently to feel the spaciousness of it. The space is there, but harder to find.

The same awarenesses apply to relationships. When flow is present between you and another person, an easeful sensation of play exists between you. Even if you are engaged in something serious, there is a sensation of *imminent* play. The play sensation is important to flow, and a peek into a children's playground will show us why:

When we watch children play, we notice that they are not concerned with time. On the time-space continuum, children at play are involved with the space end of it. They perceive their task as coming up with creative ways to use the space available to them. Even if they were wearing watches, very few children would check the time when engaged in play. On the time end of the continuum, the task is to make space fit into the chunks of time we are trying to occupy. Notice that adults, when we are rushing to meet a deadline, have little sense of play about the enterprise. When we're at the other end of the time-space continuum—keenly aware of time—there is little space in us for play.

Now, back to my ankle. I can feel more flow in my right ankle because there is more of a willingness to play in it, and more space in which to play. When we've been wounded (my left ankle is martyr to an overzealous golf swing three weeks ago), we don't feel much like playing. Let me see if I can do anything right now to feel more flow in my left ankle.

First, I notice that it turns easily to the outside, but not so easily to the inside. So I play with it for half a minute, turning it back and forth in an easy manner. Then I notice that when I extend and flex it, the extension feels easy but the flexion doesn't. So I play with that dimension for a while. Now I pause to feel it again, comparing it with my right ankle. The left ankle is now more of a match for the right. Both of them feel easy, open, and alive. There is a streaming feeling of new energy in my left ankle.

One of the most important signs of health in any relationship is how much play there is between the couple. In therapy, it's always a joyful moment when I see a little playfulness break out between two people who have been struggling, sometimes for weeks or months. How does this look in real life? Let me share a dramatic example from a relationship workshop that

Kathlyn and I taught at our Santa Barbara center.

A couple, Sarah and Jonathan, volunteered to work on an issue in the center of the circle. It was just after the lunch break, and they had gotten stuck in a conflict on the walk back from eating.

> SARAH: The problem is, he's such a controller. He wants to organize every moment of my existence.

> JONATHAN: Aw, that's ridiculous. All I said was, why not run over to the store and get the stuff we need—

> SARAH: And I wanted to have some time just to take a walk, get a breath of fresh air.

> ME: Jonathan, I notice your energy is all bunched up in your shoulders. And Sarah, you seem to be shrinking back.

> SARAH: That's him—he's like a bull.

> JONATHAN: That's ridic—

> ME (interrupting): Jonathan, instead of defending yourself, go in the other direction—be more of a bull. Bunch your shoulders up more. Sarah, shrink back more . . . really look like you're afraid.

Jonathan starts swaggering around the room like a bull, and Sarah rolls up in a tiny ball and cowers.

> ME: Let out some bull sounds, Jonathan.

> He roars lustily two or three times. She shrinks back even
> more.
>
> ME: Sarah . . . see if you can think of other ways to deal with
> bulls, rather than shrinking and getting scared.
>
> She pauses and thinks. Suddenly she brightens and makes
> like she has a bullfighter's cape. She whirls it around and teases
> him with it. He catches the spirit of the game, roaring and
> charging the imaginary cape. Soon they're involved in a full-
> fledged imaginary bullfight, with the other fifty or so people in
> the room roaring their approval when a particularly good
> move is made. After a while, both of them collapse in
> exhaustion on the carpet.
>
> THE GROUP SHOUTS IN UNISON: Bravo!

The surest sign of mental health is a healthy sense of
humor. When we can play with the things that formerly
plagued us, we're on the road to a better relationship with
ourselves as well as others.

Now, let's "flow" on to our third key feeling . . . *fear.*

Fear: The General Contractor

Fear causes contraction, especially in the middle of our
bodies. If you were watching the inside of your stomach at
the moment you got scared, you would see it turn white.
This is one of the first things that happens when we feel fear,
and if you understand why fear does this to us, you'll see why
it has such a powerful effect on our actions. Whenever we
feel threatened, even if the threat is manufactured by our
own minds, we go through a sequence of moves that we've

inherited from a long line of ancestors, most of whom had more hair on their bodies than we do.

When the fear switch is pulled:

- Blood rushes away from your stomach, and your digestion brakes to a halt. (That's what the blanching of the inside of your stomach is all about.) Since digestion consumes a large amount of energy, our ancestors evolved by being able to stop digesting food and use their energy to deal with whatever threat they faced.

- Blood rushes to the "pumps" of your body, your heart and lungs. This fuels you for fighting or fleeing.

- Your muscles get tense and ready for action.

- Your pupils narrow.

- There is a feeling of overall contraction, as if you're battening down the hatches.

The net effect of all this? Some people describe it as "butterflies," others as an inner icicle, some as "pulse-pounding panic." The common sensation is a speedy, slightly nauseated feeling that my medical colleague David Hubbard calls "racy-queasy." This feeling ranges in intensity from barely noticeable nervousness to flat-out panic.

The trigger is any threat. Don't worry about whether the threat is physical or psychological, real or imaginary. Put your attention on determining whether you feel this sensation. And if you do, learn to make the Miracle Move that relieves fear: Resonate consciously with the body sensations you're feeling, then communicate the simple truth about what you're afraid of (if there's a sympathetic ear nearby). If you're alone, resonating with the sensations of fear for ten seconds will often make them disappear.

Let me give you an example of how fear can be diminished quickly with the Ten-Second Miracle. I got a call one evening from a producer at the David Letterman show. One of my clients, a singer, had seized up with stage fright as the time for taping grew imminent. She had appeared successfully on the show several times before, but this night she would be performing a duet with another singer. Could I talk to her and find out what was wrong?

Although our conversation lasted ten minutes or so, I'll reconstruct only the key minute or two in which the Ten-Second Miracle came into play:

> ME: Are you standing up or sitting down? (I'm trying at first simply to get her attention focused on her body rather than on her runaway thoughts.)
>
> HER: Standing up.
>
> ME: *Put your attention on where your feet can feel in contact with the floor.* Are you wearing shoes?
>
> HER: Boots.
>
> ME: Okay. Feel where the soles of your feet are in contact with the soles of your boots and how those are in contact with the floor.
>
> HER (letting out a huge breath): Whewwww.

ME: Then *put your attention on where you can feel the fear in your body.*

HER: All over.

ME: Keep your attention focused on the sensations until you can feel where they're strongest.

HER: Aaah. Okay, *I can feel my heart pounding and my belly's tight.*

ME: All right. Feel those sensations and breathe into them for ten seconds. I'll count. (I count slowly to ten.)

HER: Okay. Better.

ME: Good. Tune in and feel what this may be about. Like why you might be feeling this fear right now.

HER: Yeah, I got it. [The other singer] and I had a big fight. We're singing his song, too . . . one he wrote. *I'm afraid I'll show my anger at him—won't be able to control it.*

ME: Oh, okay. So *take ten seconds and feel all your anger at him.* The fight, singing his song, the whole thing.

(I count slowly to ten.)

ME: How's that now?

HER: No big deal.

ME: Yeah. You're mad. You're scared. So what?

HER (laughs): Yeah.

I made a point to stay up late that night so I could see the results. They did a fine job.

Remember This

Once you face your fear (or any other feeling) consciously, any move will do. You can breathe into your feelings, dance with them, or speak about them with wonder. Facing into our feelings is the miracle that puts a stop to their annoying quality. Feelings all work the same way: Feel them and you heal them.

Face what you feel and you immediately begin to heal. Feel the residue of the past in your body and you put the past in its place, right where it's been all along: nowhere.

THE TEN-SECOND MIRACLE IN ACTION

Three Questions That Will Change Your Life

Questions are powerful medicine, and the right question at the right time can be the most powerful of all medicines. Questions are essential healing tools—not only for healing relationships but also for healing the body and soul. Three questions are so important to our well-being that I cannot imagine living or working without them.

I use the three questions every day in my own life. I live with them as daily companions, to keep the flow of breakthroughs coming in my marriage, my work, and my circle of friends. I use them as primary miracle workers in my professional life. I've taught them to thousands of people the world over, and I've seen them work miracles from Cleveland to Calcutta, from Belfast to Beverly Hills.

To get the full power of these three questions, take one of your current relationship problems as a test case. Think of some crucial relationship issue that's been bothering you.

Perhaps you have lost a significant love.

Perhaps you are alone and feeling lonely.

Perhaps you are in a loveless marriage.

Wherever you are, pause and think of the single most urgent relationship problem you have.

Keeping the issue in mind, ask yourself the first Key Question:

Regarding this issue, what do I most need to face right now that I've been avoiding?

Ask the question and pause until you get an answer.

Perhaps you've been avoiding . . .

- Facing and feeling a particular emotion—sadness, fear, anger—in all its depths.

- Facing the reality of a loss.

- Facing the ramifications of a choice you've made.

- Having a conversation you need to have.

Whatever it is that you've been avoiding, go ahead and face it now. Name it and face it and look at it unflinchingly for ten seconds. You don't have to do anything about it right now . . . just face it squarely.

If you face it steadily, you will feel a shift inside within not too many seconds. The shift is an inner release that's also a relief.

What you are facing may be dreadfully unpleasant. In my own life I've had to face the death of loved ones, the betrayal and loss of someone I was deeply in love with, and a number of other acutely painful events. And yet, my life seems remarkably blessed with fortune compared with the lives of many of my clients. I've sat with people as they faced sexual assault and abuse by loved ones, torture at the hands of Nazi camp guards, the murder of beloved children, and other events that go beyond my personal experience. It doesn't matter what it is we haven't faced—it's meaningless to compare the depth of one person's pain to the depth of another person's pain. All that matters is that we face what we have not faced. Almost all our symptoms and bad habits are attempts to distract ourselves from facing that one thing that must be faced.

Facing it squarely sets the stage for the second Key Question:

What is the essential Ten-Second Communication I haven't said, the one word or sentence that absolutely must be spoken?

Name it and name the person it must be spoken to. It doesn't matter if the person is sitting next to you at this moment or has been dead a dozen years. There is a Ten-Second Communication locked up inside every issue that troubles you, and the sooner you speak it the sooner you'll be free.

On several occasions, I have seen chronic illness start melting from people's bodies within hours after they spoke their truth. On one of the most thrilling occasions of my life, a woman's hearing returned, after years of deafness, following the communication of her Ten-Second truth. Often, physical problems lock into our bodies when we fail to speak that one essential truth. The problems can continue for decades until the words are finally given air.

And now the third Key Question:

What is your passion?

What do you most deeply want? What heart desire is

locked in the center of this issue that confronts you? A thwarted passion is trapped in the heart of almost every relationship problem. When we stifle our passions, we create chaos at the center of ourselves. When we live in these heartstorms for a while, our passions die and give way to despair and dull, sullen compliance.

I have worked with many people whose heartsickness was written on their faces. They were living a half-life—not quite here, not quite gone. They had suffered heart-death while their minds and bodies lived on. In each person's life, there had once been a passion, and that passion had been thwarted. It had not been nurtured and brought to light. It lay buried under layers of what one of my clients called "the silt of loss." The terrible beauty of this phrase haunts me because I was not able to help her. By the time I saw her, the passion she'd buried had begun to erode her physical body. In the same week that she came to my office, she had also visited an oncologist, who showed her pictures of the cancer that was eating her alive. For her it was too late.

I want to be sure I do not bury the passions that are sacred to me. That is what I also wish for you. Let's wake up in time by asking ourselves—by the day, by the hour, by the minute—"What is my passion?" and "Do I have the courage to express it in the world?" If we live with these questions as soul companions, the hard work of living and loving becomes heart-work.

The Three Questions in Action

Eva felt depressed and off-kilter. She also had a literal pain in the neck—a throbbing along the left side of her neck that continued

into her shoulder. I invited her to scan over her day, looking for
the first moment she could remember feeling the pain or the off-
kilter sensation. She traced it to a moment after hanging up the
phone earlier in the day.

She had hung up feeling angry about agreeing to do something she didn't want to do. Instead of using a Ten-Second Miracle in that moment, she had distracted herself by eating a
too-big breakfast, which shifted her focus to a bloated feeling in
her stomach.

I invited her to return in her imagination to that moment
after the phone call, and to ask herself two questions:

What am I not facing and feeling fully?

What is the One-Breath Communication that I need to make?

She came up with an answer quickly. She hadn't felt her
anger—her anger at herself for "being too chicken" to speak
up, and her anger at her boss on the other end of the phone.

She hadn't fully faced that she didn't want to work there any
longer, and she hadn't faced that she was afraid to quit.

I invited her to focus her consciousness on those issues for
ten seconds. I could see her visibly relax after she did that.

The One-Breath Communication she hadn't said was: *I'm
angry.* I invited her to say it out loud, then asked if she wanted
to say it to her boss. She did, so I handed her the phone. Here's
what she said:

"Is this a good time to talk about something that happened
this morning? . . . Okay, well I felt real angry this morning when
you asked me to go up to Boston and back Friday. I said I would,
but when I hung up I felt angry . . . like it was unfair to ask me
on two days' notice. I've got three kids, and it's a real chore finding someone to look after them until 9:00 on a Friday night."

She opened her eyes wide as she listened to his reply, and I must confess that I feared the worst. Suddenly she broke into a smile.

"Thanks, Jim. I really needed to hear that. And I love the idea." She hung up and let out a whoop.

Here's what he'd said: He'd been feeling guilty all day about asking her to travel on such short notice and had left a message on her home phone. He had called the other company in Boston and set up a videoconference so she wouldn't have to go in person. It turned out to be about the same cost. What made her smile break out was that he'd said there was no one else he could trust to do the job.

We didn't stop there, and I'm glad. Because there was a deeper buried treasure to be discovered.

"Eva, what is your real passion? I have the sense you could do your current job in your sleep. You seem good at it, and you get your rewards from it, but does it really represent you at your most expanded?"

She blinked rapidly.

"No," she said. "Not in any way. What I'd really like to do is take six months and immerse myself in graphic design. I want to open my own studio."

She sat down with a whoosh. "There, I've said it. Now I'm on record with it . . . I guess I'll have to do it."

I asked: "Would you be willing to trade in that 'I'll have to do it' for an 'I commit to doing it'?"

"Yes," she said.

....

Eva had to overcome many obstacles, from finances to geography, but she eventually fulfilled her passion. And if you should find your way to any of the classes offered by my organization, you'll hold many of her graphic designs in your hands. We were her first big customer.

THE FIFTH MIRACLE

*Keeping Passion Alive in
Committed Relationships*

Keeping passion alive—it's a crucial learning edge for any couple. Many people have come to my office with the question, Where did our love go? In most cases, I don't think it has gone anywhere. It just gets covered up by a shroud of unconsciousness. The real question is: What conscious moves can I make to keep love and passion flowing throughout my life? That's a question worth answering, and I have spent many years pondering it.

Kathlyn and I have been together eighteen years as of this writing. There have been many ups and downs in our relationship, but throughout our time together we have found ways to keep our passion and love for each other at a high level of vitality. I don't claim to have all the answers, but I do know what has worked for us. I can also tell you how I've used Ten-Second Miracles to help my clients maintain their passion and love.

According to my records, I've heard the following complaint more than four hundred times. Although each couple says it differently, it's the same basic complaint. Here are several versions I've lifted out of my notes:

"We don't have any fun nowadays."

"The passion has gone out of our relationship."

"We're just so used to each other. There are no surprises anymore."

"I wish we could do something to break out of our rut."

Sometimes the words are stronger, the sentiments more convoluted:

"I wish someday he would say something I haven't heard a hundred times before."

"Our sex life is so boring, the only way I can stay interested is to think about the stock market during sex."

I think you have the flavor of the problem. Unless we know how to keep passion and interest alive, we slide into a stupor of routine. Once our relationships lose their ability to surprise us, they have so little juice in them that the ups and downs of the stock market compel us more than the ins and outs of sex. When that man was 16, I doubt that he ever imagined that the price of IBM would be more interesting than sex.

What happened?

What happened to him is what happens to all of us: We lose our capacity for wonder.

In relationships, we spend every moment in one of two

states of consciousness: wonder or a trance. We are either
actively wondering about ourselves and our partners and our
potentials, or we're in a trance of routine, habits, and patterns. Some of our habits and patterns are harmless; others
hurt the hell out of ourselves and others. But that's not the
point. Whether a trance causes pleasure or pain, it's still a
trance. While we're in its grip, we are not awake to the wonderment of each moment. In other words, even if you're eating your favorite flavor of ice cream, you're not savoring it if
you're entranced while you're eating it.

I know about all this at first hand, having lived through my
share of trances. I've been fortunate to have spent much of
the past couple of decades living in wonder. Before that,
though, I spent whole years of my life in that most dangerous stupor of all: the trance in which I didn't know I was in
a trance. A trance so deep I even thought I was fully awake.
Not only have I awakened (and nodded off again) many times,
I've worked with hundreds of couples to help them wake up
to wonder. I can tell you that miracles happen when people
wake up, but I also can report that not everyone awakens
gracefully with a chirpy greeting. I include myself in that cat-
egory. On a few occasions I was so entranced that I virtually
had to be detonated out of my trance.

The trance of long-term relationship is very compelling.
There are so many pulls toward routine, so many distractions, so many comforts and pleasures to dull us. It takes a
genuine act of courage to wake ourselves up.

But if you are committed to it, you can do it. All you need is
the courage to make one key shift. The shift will take you to
the other end of the universe, but it takes less than ten seconds.

The Fifth Miracle

The Rule: *Miracles happen when you start wondering about anything you previously were sure you knew. You will see miraculous change begin in any area when you wonder about it uninterruptedly for ten seconds.*

The Move: *Wonder about anything you're worried about. Give yourself over to wondering about it for two or three full, deep breaths. Don't expect any immediate resolution ... just wonder about it with no expectations.*

Join me for a turning-point moment in my office. I'm working with Charles and Lou Ann about a money problem, as well as what they call a "basic dullness" in their relationship. They own a family business that's going through tough times. They've never incurred debt before, but now they're facing the possibility of borrowing money. This was a situation in which the Ten-Second Miracle produced an immediate financial benefit.

ME: You both look so worried. I can see all the tension about this issue bunched up on your foreheads.

LOU ANN: Yeah, it goes against our grain so much to borrow money. My grandfather started this business with twenty-five dollars and a fruit cart, and he ran it for fifty years without ever borrowing a nickel.

ME: So you're feeling guilty, too.

CHARLES: I know I am. What would the Old Man think? And I never even knew him. He died before I met Lou Ann.

LOU ANN: And we've been at each other's throats, Charlie and I.

When you work and live together, it's hard to leave it at the front door.

ME: I have a suggestion. Would you like to hear it?

LOU ANN: Sure.

CHARLES: Yes.

ME: Feel all the worry, all the guilt, all the fear you're struggling with right now. Just feel it in your bodies. Just open up to it and air it out for ten seconds.

(They close their eyes and focus inwardly for ten seconds.)

ME: Now let the worry go and shift to wondering about how this whole issue might resolve itself easefully.

CHARLES: Easefully!? (He makes a doubtful face.)

LOU ANN: I don't see how.

ME: I don't either right now—but that's what I want you to do. Wonder about it instead of worry. Worry hasn't produced any results. Try something else. Let's just wonder together for ten seconds about how this issue might work out to your advantage with ease.

(We pause for ten seconds, during which I turn my own attention to wondering about it.)

CHARLES: I have an idea.

LOU ANN: What?

CHARLES: Sell all the older trucks to raise cash so we don't have to borrow.

LOU ANN: And lease new trucks?

CHARLES: Right, short-term lease. I bet we could raise half a million dollars by selling off the old ones.

The payoff for me was immediate: I watched two people who had come in locked in worry and struggle walk out the door talking animatedly about solutions. They reported to me later that they brainstormed several new ideas before bedtime that night. The last time I heard from them, they had come through the tough times and were back in the flow again.

What You Can Do

Right now, if you are worried about why your relationship has lost vitality, shift to wondering about it for ten seconds. Adopt the wide-eyed wondering of a child. Hum a little as you're wondering. I found that if I asked my clients to hum while they were wondering, it kept them from slipping into their critical minds:

So hum a little.

Think: I wonder why things have gone flat. I wonder how I've contributed to the lack of vitality. I wonder how we might revive our vitality.

Stay out of your critical mind . . . just wonder.

You'll be amazed at the results of a few seconds of uninterrupted wonder. There's one result I can virtually guarantee you'll feel within ten seconds: Your mood will brighten and become more positive. I have yet to see a person who didn't slip into a better mood after ten seconds of uninterrupted wondering.

Why Wonder Works Miracles

When we are in a long-term relationship, we have a strong tendency to start focusing on the one or two or three parts of the relationship that don't work. There's a law of psychology that says: Whatever you focus on expands. The more we look for what's not working, the more of it we see. Then, too, the critical and judgmental part of our minds—so useful when we are diagramming sentences, reviewing plays, or repairing broken toasters—kicks in where it's of absolutely no value, in our close relationships. We become like a dog chasing its own tail. The more we criticize, the more things we see to criticize.

Often when I'm making this point in a lecture, someone in the audience stands up and says in all earnestness, "But what if you're married to someone who actually *is* wrong?" The audience typically roars with laughter, but the question points to a serious problem. We all think we're the special case, the one person in the universe who has an accurate view of reality. In other words, we all think we're the one who actually *is* right. In our rush to be right, we fail to see the obvious: Being right and being happy are at opposite ends of the spectrum. Speaking personally, I've been right and I've been happy, and I've concluded that being happy is better. Being right is a very poor substitute for enjoying a flow of loving connection with yourself and other people. It keeps us in a trance of looking for what's right and what's wrong, rather than living in wonder about how to create life in a flow of happiness, love, and contribution.

Fortunately for all of us, there is a Ten-Second Miracle that works reliably, and we have access to it all the time. I wouldn't make the following claim unless I'd seen it work countless times. I know this in my bones: A moment of pure wonder breaks the grip of the trance. Wonder is so strong, all you need is a tiny bit of it.

Listen to this moment when wonder was introduced into a relationship that had felt dead to both people for a long time.

> ME: As we talk, I feel so much sluggishness and low energy between you. It's as if both of you have been in a trance for a long time. Can you relate to what I'm saying?
>
> THOMAS: (Nods.)
>
> DORIE: Un-huh.
>
> (So little energy was being exchanged between them that it was hard to get a word out of them.)
>
> ME: Well, was there ever a time when you felt vital and passionate with each other?
>
> DORIE: Oh, yeah. When we first got together, we used to go out all the time.
>
> ME: What happened?
>
> THOMAS: You want her side of it or my side of it?
>
> ME: Maybe you can tell me your side.
>
> THOMAS: I think it was when we bought the house four years ago. I think we just got so into the routine that we lost the spark.
>
> DORIE: I don't know about that. I just got tired of always being

the one who had to take care of everything . . . while you got to do all the fun stuff out in the world.

(It was her position that he had a glamour job as a pilot; his position was that being a pilot was stressful and not at all fun.)

ME: Okay, let me ask you a blunt question. Are you willing to do whatever it takes to rekindle this relationship? So there's some life and energy in it?

They pause and blink and think. Finally they say yes.

ME: I'd like you to wonder out loud with me about how to do that.

THOMAS: How do we do that?

ME: I'll show you. Say out loud, "I wonder how we could get passion flowing again?" Both of you say it a few times— take turns just saying the question.

DORIE: *I wonder how we could get passion flowing again?*

THOMAS: *I wonder how we could get passion flowing again?*

They repeat the question a few more times.

ME: Notice the feeling that wonder produces in your body and mind? Notice how wonder feels different from worry or despair?

THOMAS: Yeah. *It feels lighter.*

DORIE: *Like opening a door and you don't know what's behind it.*

ME: Right. That's what I want you to do between now and next time you come in. Just wonder a little bit now and then. You don't have to do it all the time.

The miracle was obvious the next time I saw them. They walked in looking like they'd been plugged into a benign electric socket. Their faces appeared ten years younger. It turned out they'd stayed up until three in the morning after the previous session, talking about the twists and turns in their relationship over the preceding few years. In the course of the week they had come to a major recommitment to the passion and vital energy that had once flowed between them.

If you can catch yourself in the middle of making yourself right and somebody else wrong—if you can nab yourself in that moment and open to wonder, you will witness miracles all around you.

Wonder works especially well in revitalizing passion. Let's get specific now. Let me show you how to use wonder to keep the flow of interest and passion in long-term relationships.

Opening to Wonder

Right now, think of something you're worried about in a primary relationship. Take a few seconds and name it.

Perhaps you named it "worrying about money" or "the commitment problem with my lover." Whatever it is, just give it a name so you'll know what it is.

Now make a bold shift: Switch from worrying about it to wondering about it. However you can, drop the worry and just wonder about it. Wonder about it uninterruptedly for ten seconds.

Feel the difference in your body when you go from worry to wonder.

Wondering Is Better Than Worrying

Here are a couple of specific suggestions, drawn from examples my clients have generated:

- Instead of a worry-thought, "Are we going to have enough money to make it through the month?" rephrase it as a wonder-question: *"I wonder how we could have plenty of money to do what we want to do?"*

- Change a worry-thought such as "worrying about my lover" into *"I wonder how my lover and I can have a great relationship?"*

It might look like you're just rearranging words, but check out the different sensation in your body. When you're worrying, you're feeling fear in your body. When you're wondering, you're feeling . . . wonder! Would you rather spend your day in wonder or fear?

There's an even bigger reason for shifting to wonder, a reason that has cosmic implications. When you are worrying, you are operating in the zone of the known. No one has ever worried his or her way to happiness, prosperity, and health—worry has no space in it for any of those things. When you shift into wonder, you enter the field of possibility, leaving behind the world of limitation.

Make a little room in yourself now for wonder. Just shift worry over to the side, putting it on the back burner for a while. Open to wonder . . . you'll be amazed at what happens.

Wonder works wonders with one of the major problems of long-term relationships, and that's . . .

When Only One Person Wants to Change and Grow

Almost never do I encounter relationships in which both people are growing at the same rate. It just doesn't work that way, and there's no reason to expect that it should. We need to accept that each person has unique learning styles and rhythms. Seldom if ever do we link up with someone with the same basic pace of growth.

The situation gets sticky, however, when one person has decided to resist growth or when one person is consciously or unconsciously sabotaging the other person's growth. I've been there myself, so I know how much trouble it can cause. Kathlyn and I have been growing and thriving for nearly two decades, yet there are times when one of us is speeding up while the other is putting on brakes. Healthy relationships are never immune from the problem—they just learn to welcome it as a growth opportunity in itself.

When we find ourselves in a relationship where there is a large gap between growth rates, we are strongly inclined to point the finger of blame at the one who's driving in the slow lane. Blaming slows down the process even more, because the growth energy is then eaten up in a power struggle over who's right. As quickly as possible, we need to shift to two no-blame questions:

1. What can I learn from this situation?

2. How does my partner's approach to growth reflect some buried aspect of me that I need to look at?

Let me share an example with you of a typical break-through that these questions provide:

ME: Joyce, you've been telling us that you feel Roger is holding you back.

JOYCE: He just wants to sit on the couch and watch football! I'm sorry, but I'm at a place in my life, now that the kids are moving on toward college, that I feel like I've got to get back to me. I was a semester away from my master's when Jamie came along, and that was sixteen years ago.

ROGER: I work hard, and I like to rest my mind with football. It's probably like reading is for you.

ME: Let's step back from blaming each other for the moment. Would you be willing to do that?

They look at each other and me, then nod their heads.

ME: Okay, Joyce, I want you to do something really courageous. Let's assume that both of you are just fine; you're not right or wrong or good or bad. Rather than blaming Roger, ask yourself: How am I just like him? How is he a reflection of some part of me that I need to claim?

JOYCE: Umm. I sort of understand what you're saying, but . . .

ROGER: I think I get it. Like I'm a part of her and she's a part of me.

JOYCE: Hmm. Well, I guess Roger reflects the part of me that's not sure I can do it.

The energy shifts in the room. Roger's breathing deepens. Joyce's face softens.

ME: Say some more about that.

JOYCE: Roger is the part of me that would love to just take some time off and live in a cave for a while.

Both of them laugh.

ROGER: And she's the part of me that feels like I'm gonna die unless I get a life.

They look at each other wonderingly.

ME: So, the very thing you're complaining about in the other is something that's way down inside of you. Let's find out what you can learn from this discovery.

A key point to remember: When people are growing at different rates (or seemingly not growing at all), there is always a reason. Things don't just erode—a moment occurs when paths diverge. There was a ten-second window when something was not faced, a moment when an unconscious choice was made. When two people can pause from making each other right and wrong, they can shift to asking questions such as:

- Why is this rhythmic difference coming to light right now?

- What is this difference in growth rates trying to tell us?

- If we assumed that neither of us was to blame, what could we learn from the situation as it stands?

When people ask these questions, rapid progress can be made even if they've been bogged down for a long time. For example, a fight about toothpaste may be masking a deeper problem. There may be some real flaws in the relationship that need to be addressed. Your unconscious creates a toothpaste battle to keep you focused on trivia because you're afraid to tackle the big issues. Here are two examples of what I mean:

- One couple turned the furnishing of their house into a nightmare by fighting over the details of each little decision. Halfway through the decorating process, they came in for a counseling session. They quickly discovered that the battles over decor were camouflaging a big decision about whether to have another baby. By fighting over drapes and door handles, they were avoiding the much larger question.

- I worked with two men in their mid-twenties who were six months into the first committed relationship either of them had ever had. They were squabbling over everything from toothpaste to towel racks. When they opened up to the real issue that was driving the arguments about trivia, it turned out that neither of them had been fully open with all members of his family about his sexual orientation. As their commitment to each other grew, it brought into sharper focus the lack of communication with their original families. As you might expect, when they faced this issue and started dealing with it, the arguments over trivia stopped.

Growing at Different Rates

I've counseled well over a thousand couples who had the problem of growing at different rates. In some cases—about

10 percent—one partner outrightly sabotaged the other's growth process. An example of this is the husband who was so threatened by his wife's going back to college that he hurt his back so she had to drop out to take care of him. Later, when they worked out the issue, it took less than twenty-four hours for his back to improve so he could go back to work. Such cases are relatively rare, however. Most people I've worked with were not overtly hostile to their partner's growth process. They were just scared.

Fear is the biggest factor in differing growth rates. Many people enter close relationships with an unconscious bargain: If you won't change in any fundamental way, I won't either. If this contract remains in place, both people slide into lethargy, slumber, and routine. If the contract is broken by one partner's waking up to some new potential or desire, fear is flushed to the surface. When we're scared, we make four predictable moves.

The Four Fear Moves

When we're scared, we fight, flee, freeze, or faint. That's the way we come wired from the factory, and that's the way we're likely to be wired for the foreseeable future. This is the body we've inherited: Now, what do we do with it?

First, notice which fear move is your pattern. When you're under pressure, do you . . .

Get hostile?

Many people strike out in anger when they're really scared underneath.

Get going?

Other people withdraw and flee when the going gets tough.

Get stupid?

Many of us become confused and quit thinking clearly when we're scared. I've watched brilliant, articulate people turn into complete bumblers when gripped by, for example, the fear of abandonment.

Get spacey?

Some of us become dazed and go "out to lunch" when we're scared.

Most of us have a little bit of each of these patterns in us. Most of us, though, have one favorite pattern that we run to under stress. It's good to know what that pattern is. For me, knowing that I tend to get hostile when I'm scared helps me to take the hostility less seriously. It certainly helps my wife not take it too seriously. When I get snippy and critical, she's learned to think, He's scared about something. That's much better than what would happen early in our relationship. In those days, when I got angry, Kathlyn would often think that she'd done something wrong. Nowadays, much to my chagrin, she seldom thinks that way.

Second, get skilled at speaking directly about your fear instead of running your pattern. When I find myself getting hostile, I've learned to take a breath and speak about what's scaring me. I'm ten times better at doing that now than I was a decade ago, and I hope to be another ten times better in ten more years. It's a lifelong learning project, but it has to start somewhere. Next time you're getting angry or spacey or feeling like running away, open your mouth and force a sentence out that begins with "I'm scared that. . . ." You'll be amazed at what happens to your spaciness or your hostility or your urge to flee. I often feel the anger and tension disappear instantly from my body the moment I speak the truth of my fear.

There is another Key Rule I'd like you to consider: *The best way to inspire mutual growth in a close relationship is for each person to teach by example—not preach by conviction—the growth dimensions that are most sacred.* In other words, if reading spiritual books is a growth dimension for you, communicate your passion for them by practicing the principles in them rather than by trying to get your partner to read them. If you walked around the house ranting that your partner absolutely had to read this book, you might get it thrown at you. But if you quietly went about the practice of being in touch with your core sensations, speaking the no-blame truth, and taking full responsibility for yourself, you would find that your teaching by example had two effects.

At the very least, you would find out if you were really committed to growth or simply committed to using the techniques as a way of distancing and making your partner wrong. Some people use their own growth as a weapon to justify distancing from their partners or leaving the relationship. By your tone of voice and your attitude, you would discover if you were committed to growth for the pure exhilaration of it. That in itself would be a useful learning. The other effect, though, has some real magic in it.

Many times, if you practice your growth processes with heartful commitment, the other person slowly begins to be interested, then may become committed to the new ideas. I can give you a vivid example of this occurrence.

A woman "dragged" her husband to one of our workshops in New York. The first couple of days he was argumentative, hostile, and uncooperative. Nobody tried to talk him out of it. We just did the Ten-Second Miracles with him when he ran all his defensive strategies. He even tried to get his wife to leave the workshop, and much to her credit, she refused. On the third day, he went on a tirade about how the other fifty or so people in the room were mushy and phony and borderline unqualified to wear the title of human being. Even though he was completely obnoxious in his contempt, nobody tried to talk him out of his point of view. Later that day, he held up his hand and, from out of nowhere, blurted out, "I never believe anybody when they talk about love, because I don't know what love feels like. I put people down because it takes my mind off how much I hurt." After this electrifying One-Breath Communication, he bowed his head and sobbed. Nobody tried to talk him out of it.

I have hardly ever witnessed a more remarkable transformation. The next day he came in looking ten years younger. The wrinkles had melted from his forehead, and his cheeks had a ruddy glow. He spent the rest of the week alternating between radiant presence and heartfelt sobs. He had never bonded with his mother, having been born in wartime Europe where his family was split apart by circumstances. At one point a group of compassionate women in the workshop simply held and cradled him for an hour while he cried.

I've kept up with him over the years, and today he still has that glow. He got so turned on by the new energy he felt that he came out of retirement and took up a volunteer second career working with difficult children. I'm very proud of him, and proud to have been privy to the moment in which everything shifted for him.

THE TEN-SECOND MIRACLE IN ACTION

The Heart-Talk: A Structured Clearing Session for Solving Relationship Problems

If you've missed a number of ten-second windows over a period of time, you need a structured way of catching up and clearing the air. I've had people in my office who suddenly realized that they had a decades-long backlog of issues. Their question was, How do I begin?

The Ten-Minute Heart-Talk is an excellent way to begin. It is a structured, self-guided minisession that works extremely well *if you follow the instructions precisely.* That's a big "if," of course, because you and I both know that when people get in the heat of action, they sometimes don't follow instructions at all. That's why I recommend the Ten-Minute Heart-Talk only to people in committed relationships. I don't mean just romantic relationships—I've seen it work miracles in business, politics, and other settings. What's required is that all parties are committed to solving the problem at hand.

About half my clients turn out to be disciplined enough to make use of the Ten-Minute Heart-Talk without a third-party coach present. I usually ask people to try it out two or three times on their own at first. If they cannot do it, I recommend that they get a third person they trust to administer it and keep them on track.

The instructions are very simple, but much of the success rests on the participants' willingness to play by the rules. You begin by making a commitment to resolving the issue. Once both of you are committed, you take turns speaking uninterruptedly while the other person simply listens and takes slow, deep breaths. Following two rounds of speaking and listening, you shift to a more specific focus on feelings and sensations. Then you make the bold move of claiming responsibility for the problem and its resolution. You end by delivering validation to the other person.

The Heart-Talk is a structured beginning to what is ideally a longer discussion of the issue. The value of the Heart-Talk is that you *begin* the discussion with the communication moves that most people do not get around to. You use healthy communication moves as your jumping-off place.

You will need a timepiece with an easy-to-read second hand.

Instructions

1. Take a blank piece of paper and write a word or phrase that indicates the issue to be resolved. It can be as simple as "the budget" or "the affair" or "the dishes"— just as long as you both know what you're talking about.

Once you've written down the issue, each of you writes the following sentence and signs your name to it.

I commit to resolving the issue of _____.

(signature)

Shake hands, then put the paper away and get your timepiece with second hand.

2. Flip a coin to see who's going to be the first speaker. The other person is the timekeeper.

Minute One

Speaker

For one minute by the clock, say anything you want to say about the issue. Get to the point and say everything that needs to be said. Do your best to maintain eye contact. If you get stuck and can't think of anything to say, just deep-breathe until you think of something. Don't edit; speak spontaneously about anything that's on your mind and in your heart.

Listener

Listen, take slow deep breaths, and keep time.

Minute Two

Change roles. The speaker in Minute One becomes listener and timekeeper.

Minutes Three and Four

Do another round of exactly what you did in Minutes One and Two. Say more about the issue—anything you can think of.

Minutes Five and Six

Now, for one minute each, speak from the three core feeling zones.

Say each of the following sentences out loud, filling in the blank with whatever comes to you. Ideally, surprise yourself by what you say to fill in the blank. If nothing comes after ten seconds, say the sentence again. It is crucial that you say each sentence out loud. It is also crucial not to explain or justify why you feel however you feel. Say the feeling and move on without explaining or justifying.

> *I'm angry that _____.*
> *I'm angry that _____.*
> *I'm angry that _____.*
>
> *I'm sad about _____.*
> *I'm sad about _____.*
> *I'm sad about _____.*
>
> *I long for _____.*
> *I long for _____.*
> *I long for _____.*
>
> *I'm scared about _____.*
> *I'm scared about _____.*
> *I'm scared about _____.*

Minutes Seven and Eight

Now you will take turns taking full responsibility for the issue and your feelings about it. This is a critical step, because nothing ever gets resolved until both people take full responsibility.

The technical way this is done is to "claim cause" of each of the feelings and the issue itself. As you did in Minutes Five and Six, you will use the sentence stems to catalyze exploration.

> *I created this issue in my life because _____ .*
> *I created this issue in my life because _____ .*
>
> *I needed this issue in my life so I could _____ .*
> *I needed this issue in my life so I could _____ .*
>
> *I cause the anger I feel about this.*
> *I cause the sadness I feel about this.*
> *I cause the longing I feel about this.*
> *I cause the fear I feel about this.*
> *I set this all up so I could learn _____ .*

Minutes Nine and Ten

You end the Heart-Talk with a round of validation. With each stem, fill in the blank with a fresh appreciation.

> *I appreciate you for _____ .*
> *I appreciate you for _____ .*
> *I appreciate you for _____ .*
> *I appreciate you for _____ .*
> *I appreciate you for _____ .*

Do at least five, but continue to deliver appreciations until your minute is up.

An Example of a Heart-Talk

Dan and Perri let me watch a home video of one of their Heart-Talks. As an innovative commitment to their marriage, they gave themselves the assignment of videotaping a Heart-Talk every Thursday night at eight o'clock. They agreed to make the videotape, then watch it together holding hands. I have recommended their procedure to many couples since hearing about it.

They hold up a paper to the camera that has "Control" written on it. They each hold up another sheet that says: "I commit to resolving the issue of control." They shake hands and get out a digital watch. They flip a coin and Dan gets to speak first.

Minutes One and Two

While Perri keeps time, Dan speaks:

"I think this is more your issue than mine, but I can sort of relate, too. I mean, you say I'm controlling, but I think that you sort of do the same thing but in a different way. You criticize me for spending so much on the health club and golf and all that, and that's a way of controlling me. Your parents basically have the same sort of thing going—they are always carping at each other about how much they spend . . . you know, like your mom has to write down every penny she spends at the grocery store and all. My problem is, I don't know from week to week what you're going to be upset about. If you could just be upset about the same consistent thing, at least I'd be able to do something to figure out how to deal with it. I imagine you're talking about something specific but I don't know what—"

TIME!

Dan takes the watch and gives the floor to Perri.

She says:

"I'll tell you exactly what the issue is, very specifically. Last Wednesday I went to dinner after work, as you remember, with Donna and Marty and Paul. It was a spur-of-the-moment thing, I acknowledge that, but the fact is, I ought to be able to do spur-of-the-moment things now and then. Since Erin was born, my life seems like it doesn't belong to me anymore, so I loved the idea when they invited me to go out to dinner with them. It was like the old days, going out to celebrate a good day at work. I almost think they asked me to make me feel good, without ever having any idea I would say okay. Then when you called me on the cell phone *three times* during dinner to ask me where things were and all that, it just seemed like you were trying to own every minute of me. It got to be a joke. When's Dan going to call again? I wanted to have the time be about me and my friends, not about you and not being able to find the baby's pajama tops."

TIME!

Minutes Three and Four

They take a few deep breaths and change roles. Dan takes the floor again:

"Okay, so when I tune in to all this, I get the feeling you're really resentful that I intruded. I had what I thought were pretty good reasons for calling you, but I can kind of see what you're saying, too. So I'll think about that some more. In the meantime, though, I feel like you're hypersensitive about all this. If I try to give you any feedback at all about anything, you react like it's some kind of major criticism. Half the time, it's got nothing to do with anything major—just some little thing I'm trying to get handled. Like when I was running late for the committee meeting the other night and I asked you to help me get my stuff together, you reacted like it was such a major inconvenience. All I wanted was a little help—I wasn't trying to take over your whole evening. And when Erin was having trouble with her ear, I just suggested that maybe it was because you'd taken her out without her hat on, and you blew up like it was the end of the world."

TIME!

Perri takes the floor:

"I hate it when you ramble on like that. I'm trying to get one particular thing dealt with and you bring up a list of stuff a mile long. It's not fair. We're supposed to be talking about the issue of control. That's what I'm going to focus on. (She pauses and takes a few breaths.) Okay, so what I want is for you to look at why you might be hypersensitive too, right now, and I'll look at why I might be. But I also want you to quit trying to control and organize my time. I want some free time to myself—I don't need a whole lot, but I need to have ten minutes or a half-hour without getting interrupted by you or Erin. I'm thinking I might want to get one of those white-noise machines that make ocean-roar sounds so I can go in the bedroom now and then and get some time off. I want you to take care of Erin some time so I can do that. Really play with her without needing me for anything. I think if I can get a little of that kind of time, I might not feel so frantic all the time."

TIME!

Minutes Five and Six

Dan is the speaker:

"I'm angry that I get blamed for everything."
"I'm angry that I don't have any time for me, either."
"I'm angry that the house is never really clean
  anymore."
"I'm sad that we don't connect as much now."
"I long for walking on the beach with you."
"I'm scared that we'll just keep hassling each other."
"I'm scared we'll fight over Erin and she'll feel it."

TIME!
Perri speaks:

"I'm angry I don't have a life of my own."
"I'm angry I can't have time to sit down and read a
  book."
"I'm angry I have to go to bed at nine o'clock so I can
  get up at five with Erin."
"I'm sad I don't have enough playtime with her."
"I'm sad we don't get up to the cabin anymore."
"I'm longing for a simpler life."
"I'm longing for getting the house finally finished."
"I'm scared we won't see eye-to-eye on whether to
  have another baby."
"I'm scared you'll just keep working harder and we'll
  get further behind."
"I'm scared we won't ever feel connected again like
  we were before."

TIME!

They both pause and deep-breathe for about fifteen seconds.

Minutes Seven and Eight

Dan speaks:

> "I created this issue in my life because . . . (thinks for
> about ten seconds) . . . this is the way Mom and
> Dad lived. It's the Miller family way."
>
> "I created this issue because . . . I had no idea how
> hard it is to support a family."
>
> "I needed this issue in my life so I could . . . make up
> reasons to blame you so I don't have to be
> responsible."
>
> "I needed this issue in my life so I could . . . justify
> not wanting to have another child."
>
> "I cause the anger about all this."
>
> "I cause the sadness I feel about all this."
>
> "I cause the longing I feel about all this."
>
> "I cause the fear I feel about all this."
>
> "I set all this up so I could learn . . . patience."

TIME!

Perri speaks:

> "I created this issue in my life because . . . I'm
> exhausted all the time."
>
> "I created this issue in my life because I want to
> blame you."
>
> "I needed this issue in my life so I could . . . find out
> if you really love me."

"I needed this issue in my life so I could . . . WOW!
Justify quitting my job."

(This is a "light-bulb" moment, and she pauses to think about
it for about ten seconds. Dan is nodding his head as if to say, "I
think you're right.")
TIME!

Minutes Nine and Ten

Dan speaks:

"I appreciate you for being a great mom."
"I appreciate you for caring for me the way you do."
"I appreciate you for putting up with my habits." (He
  likes to puff an occasional cigar.)
"I appreciate you for earning $40,000 a year."
"I appreciate you for being so kind to my dad."
"I appreciate you for agreeing to marry me."

TIME!
Perri speaks:

"I appreciate you for working so hard."
"I appreciate you for wanting to live out in the
  country."
"I appreciate you for even considering having another
  baby."
"I appreciate you for staying in great shape."
"I appreciate you for cooking during the weekend."
"I appreciate you for getting up with Erin when she's
  fussy."

TIME!

I talked to Dan and Perri to get their impressions of this Heart-Talk, compared with others they'd done. They told me it was a fairly typical example, although the aha! moment, when Perri uncovered her desire to stop working, made this one stand out somewhat. They rated it a B+ (although I think they deserve an A for making the commitment to work on their relationship on a regular basis).

Each moment of our lives is an open space in which we either expand into love or contract into fear. Every moment is an ultimate window through which we greet the world with an expansive heart or a knotted stomach. Knowing this simple truth gives you a practical tool of immense value.

Consider the emotion of anger. When you are angry, you have a choice. You can shrink away from it in fear or you can embrace it with an open heart. Experience has shown me that those who spew their anger over the world do so because they shrink from it in fear. They are so afraid of anger that they must immediately get it out of their bodies, often by throwing it all over others. The cruel paradox, for them and for the rest of us, is that they end up feeling angry all the time.

The Ten-Second alternative is: Give your anger some room to breathe. Surround it with love. Tell the truth about it. Go so far as to regard it as sacred. If you can do this with something unpleasant like anger, you can easily do it with the less challenging moments of life. So let's practice on the hard stuff—our anger, our sexual feelings that intrude at inconvenient times, our late-night shudders about mortality. The exhilarating paradox is this: When we face the hard stuff and welcome it into our lives, we become free of it. When we love it just the way it is, it changes before our very eyes!

In our old state of consciousness, we feared that just the opposite was true: If we embraced it we would be stuck with it forever. Now we know that it works an entirely different way. Now we know the rules and the moves for making miracles.

Let me state them simply again, so you'll have them all in one place.

The First Miracle

You will feel a positive shift when you rest your nonjudgmental attention for ten seconds on any feeling or sensation in your body. If you rest your attention on shoulder tension, for example, you will feel it melt into flowing sensations and then to spacious openness.

The Second Miracle

You will see a miraculous change in any relationship when you speak a fundamental truth about anything real. It can be a fact, such as "I have another lover," or it can be a feeling, such as "I'm afraid you don't love me anymore." The only requirements of the communication are that it be unarguable, simple to understand, and delivered nonblamefully. Change occurs even more rapidly when the communication is a fresh discovery.

The Third Miracle

You create miraculous change when you claim full responsibility for any aspect of your life—while granting full responsibility to others. It must be pure responsibility—no fault, no
burden, and claimed freely (not because you are under pressure to do so). Commitment is a form of responsibility, and
the same rule applies. When you feel a shift to commitment—particularly about something you have previously
avoided committing to—you will see positive change in the
quality of the relationship within ten seconds.

The Fourth Miracle

Miraculous change takes place when you embrace anything about yourself or others that you have previously
shunned. When you embrace the events of the past and all
your feelings about those events, the past ceases to create
pain in your body. Change happens even more rapidly when
you love anything about yourself or others that you have previously hated. The first step is usually to love yourself for
hating it.

The Fifth Miracle

Miraculous change happens when you open your mind to
wondering about those things you've been worrying about.
You cannot wonder and perpetuate a problem at the same
time: Wonder does not exist in the same realm as problems.
As Einstein said, "A problem cannot be solved in the same
state of consciousness in which it was created." Wonder is

the ticket out of the problem realm. Ten pure seconds of it works miracles.

In Closing

I cannot express how grateful I am to have discovered what I've shared with you in this book. These concepts and practices have taught me everything I most value about life. I wouldn't be here without them. Through them, I found the miracle of my own purpose on earth. Expressing this purpose has brought me prosperity, love, and well-being. But the real miracle to me is that these ideas have allowed me the great privilege of watching thousands of people turn their lives into moving, breathing works of art in the living theater of real life. For this I will always live in grateful awe.

In this spirit, I thank you for your commitment to creating a world of better relationships. I thank you for having the courage to explore and question and invent yourself anew. I thank you for walking this far along the path with me, and I wish you every blessing on your continuing journey of miracles.